Food writer Jenny Linford's mouth-watering selection of s[...]
Small Bites & Sharing Plates such as Pesto-stuffed Mushro[...]
Dumplings and Truffle Crostini. Next you'll find satisfying *Soups & Stews* to try, like
Thai Mushroom Soup and Lamb and Mushroom Tagine. Deliciously comforting
recipes for *Grains, Rice & Pasta* include Beef Porcini Ragù with Pappardelle, Fungi
Risotto and Chickpea and Mushroom Freekeh Pilaf. *Meat, Poultry & Fish* features
more luxurious dishes like Beef Wellington, Yakitori-glazed Mushroom and Chicken
Skewers and Seabass Fillets with Shiitake Mushrooms. *Salads & Vegetable Dishes*
includes Crab, Mushroom and Fennel Salad and Mushroom Burgers and to finish
Eggs & Cheese offers relaxed recipes such as Mushroom, Blue Cheese and Walnut
Quiche and Mushroom and Parma Ham Pizza. Woven into these six recipe chapters
are informative essays, with topics ranging from meeting the mushroom growers
to fungi folklore, making this the essential cookbook for all mushroom enthusiasts.

MUSHROOMS

MUSHROOMS

deeply delicious mushroom and fungi recipes for every occasion

JENNY LINFORD

Photography by Clare Winfield

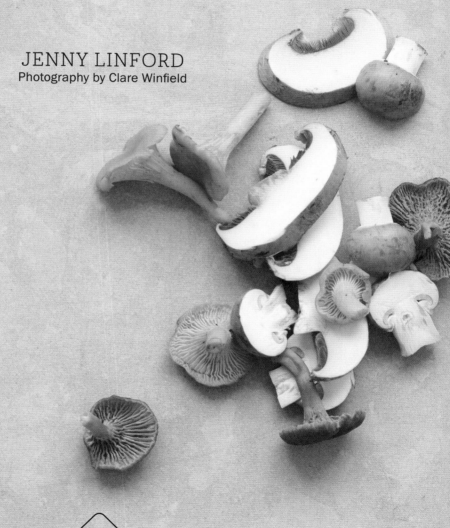

LONDON · NEW YORK

Dedication
For Chris and Ben, with my love

Senior Designer Sonya Nathoo
Editor Alice Sambrook
Picture Researcher Christina Borsi
Production Manager David Hearn
Art Director Leslie Harrington
Editorial Director Julia Charles
Publisher Cindy Richards

Food stylist Matthew Ford
Prop stylist Jennifer Kay
Indexer Vanessa Bird

First published in 2017
by Ryland Peters & Small
20–21 Jockey's Fields
London WC1R 4BW
and
341 E 116th St
New York NY 10029

www.rylandpeters.com

10 9 8 7 6 5 4 3

Text copyright © Jenny Linford 2017
Design and photographs copyright
© Ryland Peters & Small 2017

ISBN: 978-1-84975-880-2

Printed in China

A CIP record for this book is available
from the British Library. US Library
of Congress Cataloging-in-Publication
Data has been applied for.

Notes
• Both British (Metric) and American
(Imperial plus US cups) ingredients
measurements are included in these
recipes for your convenience,
however it is important to work with
one set of measurements and not
alternate between the two within
a recipe.
• All spoon measurements are level
unless otherwise specified.
• All eggs are medium (UK) or large
(US), unless specified as large, in
which case US extra-large should be
used. Uncooked or partially cooked
eggs should not be served to the very
old, frail, young children, pregnant
women or those with compromised
immune systems.
• When a recipe calls for the grated
zest of citrus fruit, buy unwaxed fruit
and wash well before using. If you
can only find treated fruit, scrub well
in warm soapy water before using.
• There is an element of risk to
ingesting wild mushrooms. The
publisher and author accept no
liability or responsibility for any
consequences resulting from the
use of or reliance upon the
information and recipes contained
in this book, nor for any health
problems, consequences or
symptoms that may arise from
contact with or the ingestion of
mushrooms, or other edible
fungi referred to herein.

CONTENTS

INTRODUCTION

There is something special about mushrooms. Humans have a long history of appreciating them; first seeking them out in the wild, then, more recently, learning how to cultivate them. As well as being an enjoyable meal, mushrooms have long been considered magical and mysterious and were used in medicine, with research today continuing to explore their healthy properties.

Nowadays, domestic cooks are lucky enough to have a wide range of fungi available to them. The charms of fresh mushrooms are subtle: their flavour is delicate, yet distinct; their texture both firm and juicy. In contrast, drying mushrooms – a process during which they shrink considerably – intensifies their flavour. Dried shiitake and porcini are both great sources of umami – the much-prized fifth 'savoury' taste – making them excellent ingredients to add to slow-cooked meat stews and braises or robust pasta sauces. Adding a few dried mushrooms alongside fresh mushrooms in dishes such as risotto or soup gives an extra 'mushroomy' flavour boost. While dried shiitake or porcini are not cheap, it's worth bearing in mind that only small amounts are needed in any dish; since they also keep well, they are worth stocking in one's store-cupboard. Similarly, dried cep or porcini powder is useful to have. Truffle oil, with its characterful, powerful taste, is another transformative flavouring, which, when used discreetly, is an effective way of adding a touch of luxury to one's food.

One of the wonderful things about mushrooms is their capacity to lift a dish – even adding just a handful to a recipe is a simple, effective way of bringing an extra dimension of flavour and texture. Needing little preparation, they are remarkably easy to cook with – one of the practical appeals of fresh mushrooms is that they cook so quickly, allowing dishes to be made in a matter of minutes. They are, of course, very good indeed eaten raw, bringing a clean, refreshing quality to salads. What struck me writing this cookbook was their versatility. Mushrooms lend themselves to so many culinary uses: simmered in soups or stews, vigorously fried over high heat, roasted, grilled/broiled, baked or just sliced and eaten. They can be an elegant presence in an aromatic soup or an appealing element in comfort food such as gratins or pies. They are used in cuisines around the world. Accordingly, in these pages you will find a globe-trotting collection of recipes from Chinese stir-fries and Indian curries to North African tagines and Italian pizza and pasta dishes. Not forgetting, of course, that much-loved classic: mushrooms on toast.

FUNGI GUIDE

When it comes to the storage and preparation of fungi, there are a few basic rules to bear in mind. Dried mushrooms should simply be stored in a cool, dark place, where they will keep well for months. Fresh mushrooms, whether wild or cultivated, are always at their best eaten as soon after harvesting as possible. As they age, their texture deteriorates noticeably and their flavour changes. Store fresh mushrooms in the fridge, but don't wrap them in plastic, as this causes them to sweat and speeds up their deterioration. Instead, let them breathe and try to use them as quickly as possible.

When it comes to cleaning fresh mushrooms, wipe them with damp paper towels or a cloth, brush them, and trim them as required. Soaking in water to wash them is not recommended, as they absorb the water and lose flavour.Do bear in mind that wild mushrooms usually require a fair bit of trimming and cleaning; use a mushroom brush or soft toothbrush to brush away the soil and dirt. Your patient work will be rewarded with flavourful results.

CULTIVATED MUSHROOMS

Progress in mushroom-cultivation techniques, based on a better understanding of the life-cycle of fungi, means that a good range of cultivated mushrooms are now available in supermarkets and greengrocers.

Buna-shimeji or brown beech mushrooms (*Hypsizygus tessellatus*): small Japanese mushrooms, with light-brown, crackle-patterned caps, valued for their firm texture. Usually eaten fried.

Button mushroom (*Agaricus bisporus*): small, white closed cup mushroom, often used whole to add texture to dishes such as casseroles and sauces.

Cremini or chestnut mushrooms (*Agaricus bisporus)*: a small, light-brown-coloured mushroom, often used whole to add texture to recipes.

Closed cup mushroom or white mushroom (*Agaricus bisporus*): white closed cup mushroom. A useful all-rounder.

Enoki (*Flammulina velutipes*): a white Japanese mushroom with a long, slender stem and tiny cap, traditionally cooked briefly, in order to preserve its flavour and texture.

King Oyster (*Pleurotus eryngii*):
a large, firm mushroom, with white stalk and brown cap; excellent for adding texture and body to dishes.

Nameko mushrooms (*Pholiota nameko*):
orange-brown mushrooms, used in Japanese cooking and classicly used in miso soup. Outside Japan, they are usually sold tinned rather than fresh.

Oyster mushroom (*Pleurotus ostreatus*):
an ear-shaped mushroom, with a delicate texture and subtle flavour. Available in different colours, including grey, pink, white, or yellow. Excellent in soups and stir-fries.

Portobello (*Agaricus bisporus*): a brown, open-capped, dark-gilled mushroom. Their size, shape and firm texture lend themselves to stuffing or using for mushroom burgers.

Shiitake (fresh and dried)
(*Lentinula edodes*): a popular Oriental mushroom with a brown cap, eaten both fresh and dried. The dried version has a noticeably meaty, umami-rich flavour.

Shiro-shimeji (*Hypsizygus tessellatus*): small white Japanese mushrooms.

Straw mushrooms (*Volvariella volvacea*): small, brown-capped mushrooms. Outside Asia, these are usually sold tinned, rather than fresh. Traditionally used in Thai Tom Yum soup.

Wood ear or Cloud ear (*Auricularia auricula-judae*): a brown, ear-shaped mushroom, usually sold dried, appreciated in Chinese and Japanese cuisine for its distinctive texture and flavour. Used in soups and braised dishes.

WILD MUSHROOMS

Particular varieties of edible wild fungi are highly prized in a number of countries for their distinctive range of flavours and textures. The fact that these varieties can't be cultivated, and so have to be seasonally foraged for, adds to their allure. Black and white truffles are one of the world's great luxuries, commanding high prices when in season. Bear in mind, if picking yourself, that wild mushrooms must be correctly identified before eating, as some are toxic. When it comes to cooking them, as with cultivated mushrooms, wild mushrooms are versatile and can be used in a number of ways.

Black truffle or Perigord truffle (*Tuber melanosporum*): a highly-prized, powerfully-scented black-brown fungus, that grows underground. Used raw or cooked to add their distinctive flavour to numerous dishes.

Chanterelle (*Cantharellus cibarius*):
a funnel-shaped mushroom, yellow in colour, with a delicate, distinctive flavour. Often used sautéed in oil or butter as a garnish for meat, poultry or fish dishes.

Chicken of the woods (*Laetiporus sulphureus*): a fleshy, fan-shaped mushroom, that generally grows in clusters. Usually eaten sautéed, either on their own or as an addition to a stew.

Field blewit (*Lepista saeva*): a pale to brown capped mushroom, nicknamed 'Blue-Leg' due to its bluish-lilac-coloured stem. Usually eaten sautéed in butter or olive oil.

Field mushroom (*Agaricus campestris*): a common brown-gilled mushroom, with a white or brown cap. Versatile – it's great fried in butter and served on toast.

Giant puffball (*Langermannia gigantea*): distinctive large, white, globe-like mushrooms. Often eaten simply sliced and fried.

Hedgehog mushroom or Pied de mouton (*Hydnum repandum*): creamy or yellow in colour with an uneven-shaped, wavy cap, with a firm texture. Often simply sautéed.

Matsutake or Pine mushroom (*Tricholoma matsutake*): prized in China, Japan and Korea, this grows under trees, including pines. A classic Japanese way of serving them is in a clear soup.

Morel (*Morchella esculenta*): a much-prized, distinctive mushroom with a cone-shaped, honeycombed cap and a distinctive flavour, varying in colour from pale brown to greyish-black. Available dried. Classically used in coq au vin.

Porcini also known as cep or penny bun (*Boletus edulis*): a highly-prized wild mushroom, with a large brown cap, thick stem and a distinctive aroma and flavour. Available fresh when in season, but usually sold dried in pieces. Fresh porcini can be simply sautéed with garlic and parsley, used in pasta or polenta sauces, or used in risotto. Dried porcini are an excellent source of intense mushroom flavour and can be used in sauces, soups, rice dishes or stews.

St George's mushroom (*Calocybe gambosa*): named for the fact that it arrives on St George's Day (April 23), ranging in colour from ivory to yellow. Use sautéed as a garnish or in soups or risottos.

Trompette or Horn of plenty (*Craterellus cornucopioides*): a dark brown to black, horn-shaped mushroom. Available dried, when it acquires an earthy flavour. Good in creamy sauces or risotto.

White truffle or Alba truffle (*Tuber magnatum*): a highly-prized, powerfully scented, pale-coloured fungus, that grows underground. In Italy, raw truffles are classically shaved over fresh pasta or beef carpaccio.

SMALL BITES AND
SHARING PLATES

JAMON AND MUSHROOM CROQUETTES

Freshly-fried croquettes are a treat. Serve this classic Spanish tapas dish with chilled fino sherry for a party nibble or as an appetizing first course, with a fresh rocket/arugula salad on the side.

20 g/¾ oz. assorted dried mushrooms (such as porcini, morels, girolles, trompettes)

25 g/2 tablespoons butter

2 tablespoons olive oil

1 leek, finely chopped

50 g/1¾ oz. Ibérico or air-dried ham, finely diced

70 g/generous ½ cup plain/all-purpose flour, plus extra for coating

350 ml/1½ cups full fat/whole milk

freshly grated nutmeg

3 eggs, beaten

100 g/1¼ cups fine dried breadcrumbs or matzo meal, for coating

sunflower or vegetable oil, for deep-frying

salt and freshly ground black pepper

MAKES APPROX. 30

Place the dried mushrooms in a heatproof bowl. Pour 400 ml/1⅔ cups of freshly boiled water over them and set aside to soak, swell and soften for 1 hour. Strain the mushrooms through a fine sieve, reserving 50 ml/3 tablespoons of the soaking water. Finely chop the soaked mushrooms.

In a large pan, heat the butter and oil until the butter has melted. Add the leek and fry gently over a low–medium heat for 1 minute, until softened. Add the ham and fry for a further minute. Mix in the flour and cook the paste, stirring, for 5 minutes to cook the flour through.

In a separate pan, heat the milk and reserved mushroom water together until hot. Gradually add the hot milk mixture to the flour paste, mixing it well with each addition.

Add in the chopped mushrooms. Cook over a low heat, stirring constantly, until the mixture thickens. Season with salt, pepper and nutmeg.

Transfer the mushroom-ham mixture to a shallow dish, cool, cover with clingfilm/plastic wrap and chill in the fridge for at least 2 hours or overnight.

Assemble the ingredients for coating the croquettes: flour for coating on a plate, beaten eggs in a shallow bowl, dried breadcrumbs on a plate. Using floured hands and working quickly, shape the chilled mushroom-ham mixture into small balls, each one the size of a walnut, rolling them on the palm of your hand. Dip each croquette first in flour, then in the beaten egg, then roll in the breadcrumbs, coating thoroughly. Place the croquettes on a tray and chill in the fridge for 30 minutes.

Heat the oil for deep frying in a saucepan to 185°C (365°F). Deep-fry the croquettes in batches for 3–5 minutes, until golden-brown on all sides. Remove with a slotted spoon and drain on paper towels. Serve at once.

MUSHROOM AND CHORIZO PICNIC PASTIES

When eating outdoors, savoury parcels that you can hold in one hand come into their own. These small pasties, filled with juicy mushrooms and spicy chorizo, encased in pastry, are a great addition to any picnic.

PASTRY
450 g/3½ cups plain/ all-purpose flour, plus extra for dusting
2 teaspoons baking powder
1 teaspoon salt
60 g/4 tablespoons lard, diced
60 g/4 tablespoons butter, diced

FILLING
1 tablespoon olive oil
1 shallot, finely chopped
1 garlic clove, chopped
100 g/3½ oz. cooking chorizo, skins cut open and discarded, sausagemeat crumbled into small pieces
300 g/10 oz. mushrooms, finely chopped
salt and freshly ground black pepper

vegetable or sunflower oil, for frying
7.5 cm/3¼ inch circular cookie cutter

MAKES 20

First make the pastry. Place the flour, baking powder and salt in a mixing bowl. Add the lard and butter and rub in with your fingertips until absorbed. Add 5–7 tablespoons cold water, mixing it in by hand to form a dough. Wrap in clingfilm/plastic wrap and chill in the fridge for 1 hour.

Meanwhile, prepare the filling. Heat the olive oil in a frying pan/ skillet. Add the shallot and garlic and fry gently over a low– medium heat for 1–2 minutes, until softened and fragrant. Add the chorizo and fry over a low heat, stirring, for 3 minutes. Add the mushrooms, increase the heat and fry, stirring often, for 8–10 minutes, until any excess moisture is cooked off. Season with salt and pepper, bearing in mind the saltiness of the chorizo. Set aside to cool.

Roll out the chilled pastry on a lightly floured surface. Cut out 20 pastry circles, using the cookie cutter. Place a teaspoon of the mushroom mixture in the centre of each circle. Brush the edges of the pastry with water and fold over the filling to form little pasties, firmly pressing the edges together to seal.

Heat the oil in a large frying pan/skillet over a medium heat. Fry the pasties in batches for approx. 5–7 minutes, until lightly browned on all sides. Remove the fried pasties with a slotted spoon and drain on paper towels. Serve warm or at room temperature.

MUSHROOM PAKORAS

There is always something irresistible about deep-fried food! These Indian-inspired pakoras – made from nutty-tasting chickpea/gram flour and flavoured with fragrant spices – are a wonderful snack, ideal for a drinks party or as the first course of an Indian meal. Serve with a herbed yogurt dipping sauce or simply with lemon wedges.

115g/¾ cup chickpea/
   gram flour
1 teaspoon ground
   cumin
1 teaspoon cumin
   seeds
½ teaspoon ground
   turmeric
½ teaspoon salt
½ teaspoon baking
   powder
½ onion, chopped
200 g/6½ oz.
   mushrooms, chopped
2–3 sprigs fresh
   coriander/cilantro,
   chopped
vegetable oil, for
   deep-frying
lemon wedges, to serve

YOGURT DIP
4 tablespoons chopped
   fresh coriander/
   cilantro or mint
   leaves
200 ml/1 scant cup
   natural yogurt

MAKES APPROX. 12–14

First, make the yogurt dip. Stir the chopped coriander/cilantro or mint into the yogurt and set aside.

Place the chickpea/gram flour, cumin powder and seeds, turmeric, salt and baking powder in a mixing bowl.

Whisk in 120 ml/½ cup water to form a thick, smooth batter. Fold in the mushrooms and coriander/cilantro.

Heat the oil in a wok or large pan until very hot. Cook the pakoras in batches, dropping in a tablespoon of the mixture for each pakora. Fry for approx. 3–5 minutes, until golden brown, turning over each pakora as it fries to ensure even browning. Remove the fried pakoras with a slotted spoon and drain on paper towels.

Serve at once with the yogurt dip or lemon wedges for squeezing.

CHAMPINONES AL AJILLO

Sometimes the simplest of things can be the best. Plump, little button mushrooms fried in garlicky olive oil, and flavoured with lemon juice, salt and parsley, are a classic tapas dish in Spain for good reason. Serve as an appetizer with chilled fino or manzanilla sherry.

6 tablespoons olive oil
2 garlic cloves, sliced across
200 g/6½ oz. button mushrooms,
    ends of the stalks trimmed
juice of ½ lemon
salt
a small bunch of fresh parsley,
    finely chopped
rustic bread, for serving

SERVES 4

Heat the oil in a heavy-based frying pan/skillet.

Add the garlic and fry until golden, taking care not to let it burn. Add the mushrooms, lemon juice and salt, mixing well. Fry briefly over a high heat until the mushrooms are lightly browned. Remove from the heat, stir in the parsley and serve at once with bread to mop up the garlicky juices.

PESTO-STUFFED MUSHROOMS

A light-textured, fragrant herb-flavoured filling works a treat in this riff on a classic mushroom dish. Serve as a first course.

4 large, even-sized field/meadow
    mushrooms, each approx. 9 cm/
    3½ in. in diameter
100 g/1⅓ cups fresh breadcrumbs
3 tablespoons pesto
3 tablespoons olive oil
25 g/⅓ cup grated Parmesan cheese
2 tablespoons pine nuts
salt and freshly ground black pepper

SERVES 4

Preheat the oven to 200°C (400°F) Gas 6.

Trim the stalks off the mushrooms and finely chop. Mix together the chopped stalks, breadcrumbs, pesto, 2 tablespoons olive oil, Parmesan cheese and pine nuts.

Brush the skin side of the mushroom caps lightly with olive oil. Place skin-side down on a baking sheet. Season the inside of the mushroom caps with salt and pepper. Fill each mushroom cap with the pesto mixture, pressing it in firmly. Drizzle the surface of the filled mushrooms with the remaining olive oil.

Bake in the preheated oven for 20 minutes and serve at once.

TRUFFLE CROSTINI

Truffle-flavoured toppings make these crostini perfect with a pre-dinner drink.

1 baguette, cut into 16 slices, 5-mm/¼-in. thick
1 tablespoon olive oil

TRUFFLED MUSHROOM PASTE
10 g/⅓ oz. dried porcini
1 tablespoon olive oil
½ shallot, finely chopped
120 g/4 oz. white/cup mushrooms, chopped
1 teaspoon brandy
½ teaspoon truffle oil
1 tablespoon mascarpone cheese
salt and freshly ground black pepper
½ tablespoon pine nuts, toasted, to garnish
chopped parsley, to garnish

TRUFFLE HONEY MUSHROOMS
80 g/3 oz. soft goat's cheese
1 tablespoon truffle honey
1 white/cup mushroom, cut into 8 thin slices
freshly ground black pepper

MAKES 16

Preheat the oven to 180°C (350°F) Gas 4.

Place the baguette slices on a baking sheet, brush lightly with the olive oil and bake for 15 minutes until browned. Set aside to cool.

For the paste topping, pour boiling water over the dried porcini; set aside for 20 minutes, then strain. Heat the olive oil in a frying pan/skillet. Add the shallot and fry gently until softened, then add the soaked porcini, mushrooms and brandy and cook over a medium heat, stirring, for 1–2 minutes. Season, then fry, stirring, until the mushrooms have softened. Set aside to cool.

In a food processor blend together the cooled mushroom mixture, truffle oil and mascarpone cheese to a smooth paste. Spread half the baguette slices with the truffled mushroom paste. Garnish with pine nuts and parsley. Spread the remaining baguette slices with goat's cheese. Drizzle each one with a little of the truffle honey and top with a mushroom slice. Season with black pepper.

MUSHROOM PÂTÉ

Serve this soft-textured pâté with oatcakes, toast or vegetable crudités.

15 g/½ oz. dried porcini
1 tablespoon olive oil
1 shallot or ½ onion, finely chopped
1 leek, thinly sliced
1 bay leaf
1 garlic clove, chopped
300 g/10 oz. Portobello mushrooms, chopped
100 g/3½ oz. cream cheese
salt and freshly ground black pepper
freshly grated nutmeg
pink peppercorns, to garnish

MAKES 350 G/1⅓ CUPS

Pour boiling water over the porcini and soak for 20 minutes until softened; drain.

Heat the olive oil in a frying pan/skillet. Fry the shallot, leek, bay leaf and garlic for 2 minutes, until the shallot and leek have softened. Add the chopped mushrooms and fry over a high heat, stirring, until they are lightly browned. Drain the mixture to remove excess moisture, discard the bay leaf and allow to cool.

Using a food processor or hand blender, blend together the mushroom mixture, porcini and cream cheese until smooth. Season with salt, pepper and nutmeg. Cover and chill. Garnish with pink peppercorns when ready to serve.

Dried mushrooms soaking

Assorted dried mushrooms

PRESERVING MUSHROOMS

With their high moisture content, fresh mushrooms can deteriorate very quickly after harvesting, so there is a long tradition of preserving them.

One historic method is to dry them. The process of driving out the moisture creates a foodstuff in which it is hard for bacteria to grow and thrive, thus allowing mushrooms treated in this way to be safely stored and eaten long after they were first gathered. Before cooking or eating, dried mushrooms are simply soaked in water to reconstitute them. The drying process intensifies and concentrates the natural flavour of mushrooms, and some dried versions of certain varieties are often highly regarded in their own right. In Chinese cuisine, for example, dried shiitake mushrooms are appreciated for their depth of flavour and robust texture. They are used in a variety of ways, for example in Buddhist vegetarian dishes, as an ingredient in braises or to flavour noodles. Another popular way of cooking with them in the Chinese kitchen is to soak whole dried shiitake, then stuff the caps with a minced pork mixture and steam them.

Precious porcini mushrooms, so beloved by the Italians, are sold dried and sliced. Only a few slices are needed to give an extra umami boost to dishes such as risottos, soups or stews, and are often used in conjunction with fresh mushrooms. Porcini paste is a popular crostini topping, served with a glass of sparkling prosecco. In Poland, dried mushrooms feature in traditional Christmas Eve dishes such as mushroom soup or borscht with mushroom dumplings. Dried mushroom powders – often cep or porcini powder – are a quick and convenient way of adding that particular umami taste to dishes.

Drying mushrooms can be done at home, either using a dehumidifier or a very low oven. Usually the mushrooms are sliced in order to speed up the process and ensure that all the moisture is removed; it is important that they are thoroughly dried out.

In Italy, another popular way of preserving mushrooms is to immerse them in olive oil, *sott' olio* (or 'under the oil'). This technique is particularly used with perishable wild mushrooms, such as porcini. The process involves salting the mushrooms, then boiling in vinegar to acidulate them, before immersing them in olive oil in order to create an anti-bacterial environment. This must be done to a high standard to eliminate any risk of botulism. Mushrooms prepared in this way are a popular element in antipasti platters or on pizzas.

In Britain, mushroom ketchup was first mentioned in cookbooks in the 18th century. Making it was quite a process, as fresh mushrooms were layered with salt and set aside for days to extract their moisture. The resulting liquor was cooked and seasoned with spices, then strained to produce a thin, salty, spicy liquid. In her 1861 *Book of Household Management*, Mrs Beeton specifies that mushrooms should be picked in dry weather, 'for if they are picked during very heavy rain, the ketchup from which they are made is liable to get musty, and will not keep long.' In her opinion, it was well worth making: 'This flavouring ingredient, if genuine and well prepared, is one of the most useful store sauces to the experienced cook and no trouble should be spared in its preparation.' Initially made domestically, the 19th century saw it also being produced commercially, with the company Geo. Watkins, founded in 1830, still producing it.

Pickling mushrooms is enjoying a revival as chefs embrace the vogue. Rather than pickling them in order to extend their shelf-life, light pickling is now used to create a distinctive tangy flavour, while maintaining the mushrooms' characteristic texture. Quick and easy to make, pickled mushrooms go well with cold meat, cheese or smoked fish platters.

Clean and trim 200 g/7 oz. button mushrooms. Place 250 ml/1 cup cider or white wine vinegar and 100 ml/ $\frac{1}{3}$ cup water in a pan with a whole peeled garlic clove, 2 crushed fresh bay leaves, 1 dried chilli/chile, 1 tablespoon coriander seeds, 1 chopped shallot and 1 teaspoon salt. Bring to the boil, add the mushrooms and boil for 2–3 minutes. Remove from the heat, cover, cool the mushrooms in their liquor and store in a clean jar, covered, in the fridge for up to a week. Remove the mushrooms with a slotted spoon to serve.

MUSHROOM VOL-AU-VENTS

That much-loved, retro party nibble, the vol-au-vent, is still popular for good reason. The combination of a light, crisp puff pastry case with a tasty filling is hard to resist. Here, the rich and creamy mushroom filling is given an umami boost with the addition of a touch of cep powder, making them especially appetizing.

12 vol-au-vent puff
   pastry cases/shells
½ tablespoon olive oil
1 teaspoon butter
1 shallot, finely chopped
150 g/5 oz.
   mushrooms, finely
   chopped
2 sprigs of thyme,
   leaves picked
150 ml/⅔ cup double/
   heavy cream
a pinch of dried cep or
   porcini powder
freshly grated nutmeg
½ teaspoon cornflour/
   cornstarch
½ teaspoon milk
salt and freshly ground
   black pepper

MAKES 12

Preheat the oven to 220°C (450°F) Gas 7.

Place the vol-au-vent pastry cases/shells on a baking sheet and bake in the preheated oven for 15–20 minutes, or according to the package instructions, until risen and golden brown. Remove from the oven and carefully cut out the excess pastry from inside each vol-au-vent.

Reduce the oven temperature to 200°C (400°F) Gas 6.

Meanwhile, prepare the filling. Heat the olive oil and butter in a frying pan/skillet. Fry the shallot gently until softened. Add the mushrooms and thyme and fry gently, stirring now and then, until the mushrooms are lightly browned. Season with salt and pepper.

Stir in the cream and season with the cep powder and grated nutmeg. Mix the cornflour/cornstarch with the milk and stir into the mushroom mixture. Cook gently, stirring, until the mixture thickens.

Spoon the mushroom mixture into the vol-au-vent cases. Return them to the oven and bake for 15 minutes until piping hot. Serve warm from the oven.

MUSHROOMS ON TOAST TWO WAYS

This way of serving mushrooms is classic for good reason. Here, I've given two versions: one rich and creamy, the other fragrant and tangy – both tasty!

LUXURY MUSHROOMS ON TOAST

25 g/2 tablespoons butter
200 g/6½ oz. mushrooms, sliced
   1-cm/½-inch thick
1 teaspoon brandy
a pinch of freshly grated nutmeg
½ teaspoon sweet smoked paprika
1 tablespoon double/heavy cream
2 slices of toast, freshly made
freshly chopped chives, to garnish
salt and freshly ground black pepper

SERVES 2

Heat the butter in a frying pan/skillet until frothing. Add the mushrooms and fry over a medium heat for about 2 minutes, until they begin to take on colour.

Add the brandy and cook, stirring, for a few seconds. Season with nutmeg and smoked paprika. Add the cream, mixing thoroughly, and cook over a gentle heat for 1–2 minutes. Season with salt and pepper.

Spoon the mushroom mixture onto the freshly made toast. Garnish with chives and an extra dusting of paprika, if you wish, and serve.

LEMON AND THYME MUSHROOMS ON TOAST

½ tablespoon olive oil
200 g/6½ oz. mushrooms, sliced
   1-cm/½-inch thick
2 sprigs of thyme
grated zest and juice of 1 lemon
1 tablespoon freshly chopped
   parsley
2 slices of toast, freshly made
cream cheese, for spreading
salt and freshly ground black pepper

SERVES 2

Heat the oil in a frying pan/skillet. Add the mushrooms and the thyme and fry over a gentle heat, stirring frequently, for 3–4 minutes. Discard the thyme.

Add the lemon zest and juice. Season with salt and pepper and stir in the parsley. Spread the toast with cream cheese, top with the mushrooms and serve.

SHIITAKE POTSTICKER DUMPLINGS

Dumplings are always popular and these are no exception! Dried shiitake mushrooms have a wonderful depth of flavour and here they are combined with spring onion/scallion, garlic and root ginger to make a truly tasty filling. Serve these as the first course of a Chinese meal or as a party nibble with drinks.

60 g/2 oz. dried
   shiitake mushrooms
2 spring onions/
   scallions, finely
   chopped
1 garlic clove, finely
   chopped
2.5-cm/1-inch piece
   of root ginger,
   finely chopped
1 tablespoon rice wine
   or Amontillado sherry
1 teaspoon soy sauce
1 teaspoon sesame oil
salt
a pinch of sugar
22 potsticker/gyoza
   wrappers
2 tablespoons vegetable
   oil, for frying

DIPPING SAUCE
3 tablespoons light
   soy sauce
3 tablespoons Chinese
   rice vinegar
1 thin slice of root
   ginger, finely chopped
½ teaspoon chopped
   red chilli/chile or
   Aleppo chilli/hot
   pepper flakes

MAKES 22 DUMPLINGS

Place the dried shiitake mushrooms in a bowl and cover with freshly boiled water. Set aside to soak for 30 minutes, weighing down the mushrooms in the bowl if necessary to make sure they soften. Drain the mushrooms. Trim off and discard the tough stems.

Place the shiitake, half the chopped spring onion/scallion, garlic and ginger in a pan. Cover with water and add the rice wine. Bring to the boil. Partly cover and simmer for 45 minutes. Drain and cool.

Place the shiitake mushrooms in a food processor and pulse until finely chopped. Mix the minced shiitake with remaining spring onion/scallion, soy sauce, sesame oil, salt and sugar.

To make each dumpling, place a heaped teaspoon of the shiitake mixture in the centre of a wrapper. Brush the edges with a little water, fold over the filling and tightly press together to seal well. Repeat the process until all the wrappers are filled.

To cook the potstickers, heat 1 tablespoon oil in a large, lidded heavy-based frying pan/skillet. Add a layer of the dumplings, flat side-down. Fry for 2–3 minutes. Sprinkle over 75 ml/⅓ cup cold water, taking care as it will splutter. Cover the pan and cook for 10 minutes over a low-medium heat. Set aside and keep warm.

Repeat the process with the remaining dumplings.

Mix together all the ingredients for the dipping sauce and serve alongside the dumplings.

MUSHROOM, BACON AND ONION PANCAKES

Starting your weekend with a proper breakfast or a late brunch always feels like a treat. These small, fluffy pancakes – flavoured with mushrooms, bacon and onion – make a great savoury all-in-one breakfast dish to enjoy. Make a tall stack of them and share with friends.

½ tablespoon
   sunflower oil
3 bacon rashers/slices,
   cut into short strips
½ onion, finely chopped
100 g/3½ oz. button
   mushrooms, halved
225 g/1¾ cups plain/
   all-purpose flour
1 tablespoon baking
   powder
½ teaspoon salt
2 eggs
200 ml/1 scant cup
   milk
1 tablespoon freshly
   chopped parsley
1 tablespoon freshly
   chopped chives
25 g/2 tablespoons
   butter, melted
maple syrup, to serve
   (optional)

MAKES APPROX.
16 PANCAKES

Heat the sunflower oil in a frying pan/skillet. Fry the bacon and onion for 2 minutes, stirring. Add the mushrooms and fry over a high heat until lightly browned. Set aside to cool.

Sift the flour, baking powder and salt into a mixing bowl. Break the eggs into the centre of the flour and pour in the milk, folding the ingredients together quickly, without over-mixing, to form a thick batter. Gently fold in the mushroom mixture, parsley and chives. Stir in the melted butter.

Thoroughly heat a large, heavy-based frying pan/skillet. Dry fry the mixture in batches, using a tablespoon of the batter to form each small pancake. Fry for 2–3 minutes over a low-medium heat, until the pancakes have set and begun to dry out around the edges. Using a spatula, gently turn them over and fry for a further 2 minutes until golden brown on both sides. Serve at once.

MUSHROOM-FILLED LETTUCE CUPS

Light and elegant, with pleasantly contrasting textures, these filled lettuce leaves make an appealing first course. Alternatively, serve them as a drinks party nibble. Fresh oyster or shiitake mushrooms would work well in this Chinese-inspired dish. Similarly, radicchio or chicory leaves, with their distinctive bitter note, could be used instead of lettuce.

1 tablespoon vegetable oil

1-cm/½-inch piece of root ginger, finely chopped

1 garlic clove, finely chopped

2 spring onions/scallions, finely chopped, separated into white and green

300 g/10 oz. white/cup mushrooms, cut into 1-cm/½-inch dice

1 tablespoon rice wine or Amontillado sherry

2 teaspoons light soy sauce

1 tablespoon oyster sauce

8 even-sized Little Gem lettuce leaves

coriander/cilantro sprigs, to garnish

finely chopped red chilli/chile, to garnish

MAKES 8

Heat the oil in a wok or large frying pan/skillet. Add the ginger, garlic and white spring onion/scallion and stir-fry over a medium heat for 1 minute.

Add the diced mushrooms and stir-fry for 2 minutes. Add the rice wine or sherry and stir-fry for 1 minute, until cooked off. Add the soy sauce and oyster sauce. Stir-fry for 2 minutes. Toss through the green spring onion/scallion.

While the mushroom mixture is hot or at room temperature, spoon it into the lettuce leaves, filling each one with the mixture.

Garnish with coriander/cilantro leaves and finely chopped red chilli/chile and serve at once.

SOUPS
AND STEWS

MUSHROOM AND BEAN CHILLI

This spicy vegetarian take on a classic chilli con carne is both simple and quick to make. It can also, usefully, be made a day in advance and kept in the fridge until needed. Serve with freshly baked cornbread, warm from the oven, or baked potatoes. It's especially good with tangy sour cream, which contrasts nicely with this rich tomato-based dish.

1 tablespoon olive oil
1 onion, chopped
1 garlic clove, chopped
1 celery stalk, chopped
½ red (bell) pepper, finely chopped
150 g/5 oz. field mushrooms (Portabellini), finely chopped
1 teaspoon ground cumin
pinch of dried oregano
½ teaspoon smoked paprika
1 x 400-g/14-oz. can of chopped tomatoes
1 teaspoon chipotle paste

pinch of sugar
1 x 400-g/14-oz. can of kidney beans in water, drained and rinsed
200 g/6½ oz. button mushrooms, halved if large
salt and freshly ground black pepper
freshly chopped coriander/cilantro, to garnish
sour cream, to serve
grated Cheddar cheese, to serve

SERVES 4

Heat the oil over a medium heat in a casserole dish or Dutch oven. Add the onion, garlic, celery and red (bell) pepper and fry, stirring, for 5 minutes until softened. Add the field mushrooms (Portabellini), cumin, oregano and smoked paprika and fry, stirring, for 5 minutes.

Add the chopped tomatoes, 200 ml/1 scant cup of water, chipotle paste and sugar. Season with salt and pepper and stir well. Bring to the boil, then stir in the kidney beans and button mushrooms.

Lower the heat to medium and simmer, uncovered, for 15 minutes, stirring now and then. Portion into bowls and garnish with the chopped coriander/cilantro. Serve with sour cream and grated Cheddar cheese, if desired.

THAI MUSHROOM SOUP

A clear, flavourful broth, with appealing citrus notes, which showcases the tender texture of fresh mushrooms.

2 lemongrass stalks
200 g/6½ oz. assorted oyster, shimeji and button mushrooms; if unavailable use button mushrooms
1 tablespoon olive oil
1 onion, chopped
2.5-cm/1-inch piece of root ginger, chopped
1 litre/4 cups good quality chicken stock/broth
4 kaffir lime leaves
2 fresh red chillies/chiles
2–3 tablespoons fish sauce, or to taste
juice of ½ lime or ½ lemon
a handful of fresh coriander/cilantro, to garnish
salt

SERVES 4

Trim the lemongrass stalks of their tough outer casing. Finely chop the soft, lower, bulbous white part of each stalk. Slice the oyster mushrooms and button mushrooms.

Heat the oil in a large saucepan over a medium heat. Add the onion, ginger and lemongrass and fry, stirring, for 1–2 minutes until the onion has softened and the mixture is fragrant. Add the stock/broth, lime leaves and whole chillies/chiles. Season to taste with salt.

Bring to the boil. Add the fish sauce and lime juice. Taste to check the seasoning; you want a salty, tangy flavour. Bring the soup to the boil once more. Add the mushrooms, then lower the heat and simmer for 2 minutes until just tender. Ladle into bowls and serve at once garnished with the fresh coriander/cilantro.

MISO MUSHROOM SOUP

A wonderfully quick, Japanese-inspired light lunch or supper – so perfect when you need a meal in a hurry!

10 g/⅓ oz. instant dashi stock powder
900 ml/4 cups boiling water
1 tablespoon red miso paste
1 teaspoon vegetable oil
1-cm/⅜-inch piece of root ginger, chopped
1 spring onion/scallion, finely chopped
a dash of mirin or dry sherry
50 g/⅓ cup green beans, cut into short lengths
150 g/5 oz. assorted fresh shiitake, oyster and shiro-simeji mushrooms, the shiitake sliced 1-cm/⅜-inch thick

SERVES 4

Mix the dashi stock powder into the boiling water and stir until dissolved. Mix 3 tablespoons of the hot dashi stock with the miso paste to thin it out. Set both aside.

Heat the oil in a large saucepan over a medium heat. Fry the ginger and sliced white part of the spring onion/scallion, stirring, for 1 minute. Add the dashi stock, a dash of mirin or dry sherry and the thinned miso paste, stirring it in well. Bring to the boil, then stir in the green beans and assorted mushrooms.

Simmer for 3–5 minutes; you want the mushrooms and the green beans to retain their texture. Portion into bowls and serve at once, garnished with the green part of the chopped spring onion/scallion.

2 tablespoons olive oil

700 g/25 oz. braising
  beef, cubed

2 onions, chopped

2 garlic cloves, chopped

1 celery stalk, finely
  chopped

1 bay leaf

3 sprigs of fresh thyme

500 ml/2 cups Chianti
  red wine

400 ml/1²/₃ cups beef
  stock/broth

25 g/1 oz. dried porcini
  mushrooms, soaked
  in warm water for
  20 minutes, drained

½ celeriac, peeled
  and cubed

2 carrots, peeled and
  cut into chunks

2 teaspoons butter

100 g/3½ oz. wild
  mushrooms or
  6 white/cup
  mushrooms, halved

salt and freshly ground
  black pepper

DUMPLINGS

115 g/³/₄ cup plus
  2 tablespoons
  self-raising/self-rising
  flour

50 g/3 tablespoons
  suet or lard

a pinch of salt

2 tablespoons porcini
  powder (cep powder)

SERVES 6

CHIANTI AND BEEF CASSEROLE WITH PORCINI DUMPLINGS

Rich and succulent, this splendid stew makes a great dish for entertaining. If need be, cook the casserole a day in advance, then make and add the dumplings on the day of serving.

Preheat the oven to 150°C (300°F) Gas 2.

Heat 1 tablespoon of the oil in a large casserole dish or Dutch oven over a high heat. Add the beef and fry until browned on all sides; remove.

Add the remaining oil over a medium heat to the same dish. Add the onion, garlic, celery, bay leaf and thyme sprigs and fry for 3 minutes until the onion has softened and the mixture is fragrant. Return the beef to the dish and mix in with the other ingredients. Pour in the Chianti red wine and beef stock/broth. Season with salt and pepper.

Add the soaked porcini, celeriac and carrots. Bring to the boil. Cover and transfer the casserole to the preheated oven. Bake for 1½ hours until the meat and vegetables are tender.

To make the dumplings, mix together the flour, suet or lard, salt and porcini powder in a mixing bowl. Mix in 100–120 ml/7–8 tablespoons of cold water to form a soft, sticky dough. With wet hands, shape into 12 small, round dumplings.

Add the dumplings to the stew, cover and return to the oven for a further 30 minutes, until soft and plump.

Shortly before the dumplings are ready, heat the butter in a small, heavy frying pan/skillet and fry the wild mushrooms or white/cup mushrooms over a medium heat until just softened and lightly coloured. Stir the fried mushrooms into the casserole before serving.

FUNGI FACTS

Mushrooms and truffles both belong to the large and fascinating family of organisms we call Fungi. Neither plants nor animals, various types of fungi are uniquely classified as a 'kingdom'. There are an estimated 1.5 million species of fungi, although only about 100,000 have been properly chronicled.

Fungi play a huge part in our lives. They perform an invaluable role in our planet's natural environment by breaking down organic matter, so recycling nutrients. From a culinary point of view, fungi are essential to many foods and drinks we enjoy. The baker's yeast that causes our bread to rise, the brewer's yeast with which beer is made and the *Penicillium roqueforti* mould used to create blue cheeses, are all fungi.

Mushrooms are the fruiting bodies of a fungus, which, in fact, forms a much larger living organism; one analogy is to think of them as being like apples on a tree. Mushrooms are formed by a fungus to distribute the spores by which it will reproduce. In contrast to the visible mushrooms, the main part of the fungus, known as the mycelium, is hidden from sight. This is made up of tiny, fine filaments called hyphae, which spread and mesh together to create the mycelium, through which the fungus feeds. The fungus releases enzymes that allows them to break down nutrients, thus, as they can't move, they always grow in and on their food source. Certain types of fungi, among them highly prized truffles, ceps and chanterelles, grow with mature trees, creating

Honey fungus (*Armillarilla mellea*)

Golden jelly fungus (*Tremella mesenterica*)

Bleeding fairy helmets
(*Mycena haematopus*)

Common puffballs (Lycoperdon perlatum)

Velvet shank (*Flamminula velutipes*)

a mutually beneficial relationship with their roots, making it hard to cultivate them commercially.

The Fungi family contains a diverse range of sizes, from single-cell organisms to large fungi. In fact, the largest living thing on our planet is thought to be a huge honey fungus (*Armillaria solidipes*) growing in the Blue Mountains, Oregon, USA, that covers an area of 3.7 square miles (9.6 square kilometres). Estimates of its age vary from between 2,400 years old, based on its current growth rate, to nearly 9,000 years old. Furthermore, the formations that fungi assume vary hugely. Mushrooms themselves come in a variety of colours: blue, red, yellow and orange, as well as the better-known white and brown. Shapes range from the familiar 'umbrella' shape to more unusual ones, such as the appropriately-named shaggy 'lion's mane' or the gnarled 'brain' mushroom. The way in which fungi spread their spores also varies. The giant puffball fills with powdery spores as it ages and, when mature, the outer skin bursts. Passive airborne dispersal such as this is a common way in which spores are spread. Certain fungi, however, such as the cannonball fungus, actively discharge their spores. Stinkhorn mushrooms exude a slime that smells of rotten flesh, which attracts flies to disperse their spores. Truffles, similarly, attract animals to them through a powerful odour. When eaten, however, the truffle's spores remain undigested, so pass through the animal and are accordingly dispersed.

Mushrooms have been used in ancient medicine for centuries. Certain fungi have antibiotic properties, most famously penicillin, which was developed by Alexander Fleming from a mould. It is now realized that many fungi possess antibacterial and antiviral compounds, the thinking being that once a mycelium has been created by a fungus, it produces toxins to keep other fungi away and protect its food. In the scientific community, there is much interest in researching the potential of fungi in areas such as the cleaning up of pollution and radiation and their anti-cancer and immune-boosting properties.

MUSHROOM SOUP

2 tablespoons sunflower
   oil
½ onion, chopped
1 leek, finely chopped
a sprig of thyme,
   leaves only
500 g/1 lb. field
   mushrooms, stalks
   trimmed and
   chopped
1 potato, peeled
   and diced
a splash of Maderia or
   Amontillado sherry
700 ml/3 cups good
   chicken stock/broth
freshly ground nutmeg
salt and freshly ground
   black pepper
1 tablespoon olive oil
200 g/6½ oz. chestnut/
   cremini mushrooms,
   sliced, to serve
double/heavy cream,
   to garnish
freshly chopped chives,
   to garnish

GARLIC CROUTONS
2 tablespoons olive oil
1 garlic clove, peeled
2 slices of day-old
   rustic bread, crusts
   trimmed off, cut into
   small cubes

SERVES 4

There is something very comforting about a good mushroom soup, with its particular earthy flavour and smooth richness. Here, garlicky croutons and freshly-fried chestnut/cremini mushrooms are a very simple but effective way of adding a flavour and texture boost to this classic soup.

Heat the sunflower oil in a large saucepan over a medium heat. Add the onion, leek and thyme leaves and fry gently, stirring now and then, for 5 minutes until softened. Add the field mushrooms and fry, stirring, for 3 minutes until lightly browned.

Mix in the diced potato, then add the Madeira or sherry and cook, stirring, for a minute. Pour in the chicken stock/broth and bring to the boil. Reduce the heat, cover and simmer for 25 minutes.

Meanwhile, make the croutons. Heat the olive oil in a frying pan/skillet over a medium heat. Add the garlic clove and fry briefly until fragrant. Add the cubes of bread and fry until golden-brown and crisp, discarding the garlic clove when it browns.

Purée the cooked soup until smooth in a food processor or using a stick blender. Season with salt, freshly ground pepper and nutmeg. Bring to a simmer again in the pan to heat through.

When ready to serve, heat 1 tablespoon of olive oil in a frying pan/skillet over a medium-high heat. Fry the chestnut/cremini mushrooms until lightly browned.

Serve the warm soup in bowls, garnished with a swirl of double/heavy cream, some hot fried mushrooms, garlic croutons and chopped chives.

LAMB AND MUSHROOM TAGINE

This slow-cooked lamb and vegetable tagine is simple to make and very pleasant to eat. Flavoured with a base of fragrant spices, the mushrooms are added towards the end of the cooking time and simmered only briefly so as to retain their firm bite. You can serve this with buttered couscous, quinoa or basmati rice, offering harissa on the side for a touch of piquancy.

1 tablespoon
    sunflower oil
1 tablespoon butter
1 large onion, finely
    chopped
½ cinnamon stick
1 teaspoon cumin
    seeds
½ teaspoon ground
    cinnamon
½ teaspoon ground
    ginger
500 g/1 lb. lamb neck
    fillet, cubed
2 tablespoons tomato
    purée/paste
2 turnips, diced
2 carrots, peeled and
    cut into chunks
250 g/8 oz. white/cup
    mushrooms, halved
salt and freshly ground
    black pepper
freshly chopped
    coriander/cilantro,
    to garnish

SERVES 4

Heat the oil and butter in a casserole dish or Dutch oven over a medium heat. When the mixture begins to froth, add the onion, cinnamon stick, cumin seeds, ground cinnamon and ginger. Fry briefly, stirring, for 2 minutes until fragrant. Mix in the lamb, coating well in the spices.

Stir in 900 ml/3½ cups water, the tomato purée/paste, turnips and carrots. Season with salt and freshly ground black pepper.

Bring to the boil, then reduce the heat, cover and simmer for 1 hour until the lamb is tender.

Bring to the boil again, add the mushrooms and simmer for 5 minutes. Serve at once, garnished with the chopped coriander/cilantro.

MUSHROOM, SPINACH AND COCONUT CURRY

If you've come home after a long, busy day and want to make something speedy but tasty for supper, this mellow yet aromatic curry hits the spot! Both mushrooms and spinach require very little cooking, so this is gloriously quick to make. Serve with perfumed basmati rice, naan or paratha flatbreads for a delicious taste of the tropics.

1 tablespoon sunflower oil
1 teaspoon mustard seeds
1 onion, finely chopped
2.5-cm/1-inch piece of root ginger, finely chopped
2 garlic cloves, chopped
½ cinnamon stick
4 cardamom pods
2 teaspoons ground coriander
2 teaspoons ground cumin
½ teaspoon ground turmeric
¼ teaspoon chilli/chili powder
1 x 400-ml/14-oz. can of coconut milk
400 g/14 oz. white/cup mushrooms, halved
250 g/8 oz. fresh spinach
salt and freshly ground black pepper

SERVES 4

Heat the sunflower oil in a casserole dish or large, heavy saucepan over a medium heat. Add the mustard seeds and fry briefly until they begin to pop. Add the onion, ginger, garlic, cinnamon stick and cardamom pods and fry gently for 5 minutes, stirring often, until the onion has softened and the mixture is fragrant.

Meanwhile, quickly mix together the coriander, cumin, turmeric and chilli/chili powder with 2–3 tablespoons of water to form a spice paste.

Add the spice paste to the onion mixture. Fry, stirring, for 1 minute. Add the coconut milk and stir while bringing to the boil. Add the mushrooms and simmer for 5 minutes. Mix in the spinach and cook briefly until just wilted. Season with salt and pepper and serve at once.

TOFU AND MUSHROOM HOTPOT

Mushrooms and tofu have a natural affinity as ingredients, and they are combined here in a fresh vegetarian take on a classic Chinese hotpot. Serve with steamed rice or boiled noodles for lunch or supper.

400 g/14 oz. firm tofu, well drained
8 dried shiitake mushrooms
1 tablespoon cornflour/cornstarch
2 tablespoons vegetable oil
½ onion, chopped
1 leek, finely sliced
2.5-cm/1-inch piece of root ginger, finely chopped
1 garlic clove, chopped
¼ head of Chinese leaf/napa cabbage, roughly chopped
3 tablespoons rice wine or Amontillado sherry
a pinch of Chinese five spice powder
150 g/5 oz. assorted fresh mushrooms (oyster, shiitake, eryngii), large ones halved
1 tablespoon light soy sauce
pinch of sugar
1 teaspoon sesame seed oil
salt
chopped spring onion/scallion, to garnish

SERVES 4

Wrap the tofu in paper towels and place a weighty item (such as a heavy baking sheet) on top. Leave for at least 10 minutes to let the excess moisture drain.

Soak the dried shiitake mushrooms in 200 ml/1 scant cup of hot water for 20 minutes. Strain through a fine-mesh sieve/strainer, reserving the soaking liquid. Trim and discard the tough stalks from the shiitake and cut them in half.

Cut the tofu into cubes and roll them in the cornflour/cornstarch to coat. Heat 1 tablespoon of the oil in a frying pan/skillet. Fry the tofu for 5 minutes over a medium-high heat, turning over during frying, until lightly browned on all sides.

Heat the remaining oil in a casserole dish or Dutch oven over a medium heat. Add the onion, leek, ginger and garlic and fry, stirring, for 2 minutes. Add the Chinese leaf/napa cabbage and fry for a further 2 minutes. Mix in the rice wine or sherry and five spice powder and cook for 1 minute. Add the fried tofu, soaked shiitake and the fresh mushrooms.

Pour in the reserved shiitake soaking liquid, soy sauce and add the pinch of sugar. Bring to the boil. Cover and cook over a medium heat for 15 minutes. Uncover and cook for 10 minutes, stirring gently now and then. Season with salt. Stir in the sesame seed oil. Serve straight away, garnished with chopped spring onion/scallion.

MUSHROOM, PANEER AND PEA CURRY

This quick vegetarian curry is an ideal midweek meal. Among its charms is a pleasing combination of textures, with the crisp fried firmness of paneer cheese contrasting nicely with the tender mushrooms and peas, all coated in a spiced, creamy tomato sauce.

450 g/15 oz. paneer
  cheese, cut into
  2.5-cm/1-inch cubes
½ teaspoon ground
  turmeric
3 tablespoons vegetable
  oil
1 cinnamon stick
1 onion, chopped
2.5-cm/1-inch piece of
  root ginger, chopped
1 garlic clove, chopped
.3 teaspoons ground
  cumin
2 teaspoons ground
  coriander
½ teaspoons chilli/chili
  powder
1 x 400 g/14-oz. can
  of chopped tomatoes
½ teaspoon sugar
300 g/10 oz. white/cup
  mushrooms, halved
300 g/2 cups of frozen
  peas, defrosted
3 tablespoons double/
  heavy cream
salt and freshly ground
  black pepper
freshly choppped
  coriander/cilantro,
  to garnish

SERVES 4

Place the paneer chese in a bowl and sprinkle with ¼ teaspoon of the turmeric. Toss to coat the cheese lightly and evenly on all sides. Heat 2 tablespoons of the oil in a large, heavy frying pan/skillet. Fry the cheese in the oil over a medium heat until lightly browned on all sides. Remove and set aside.

Add the remaining oil to the pan and heat through. Add the cinnamon stick, onion, ginger and garlic and fry over a low heat, stirring often, until the onion is lightly browned.

Meanwhile, quickly mix together the cumin, coriander, chilli/chili powder and remaining turmeric with a little water to form a paste. Add the spice paste to the frying onion and cook gently, stirring, for 2 minutes.

Add the chopped tomatoes, mixing in well. Season with salt and freshly ground black pepper and mix in the sugar. Bring to the boil. Add the mushrooms, peas and fried paneer and cook, stirring now and then, for 10 minutes over a medium heat. Stir in the double/heavy cream. Serve at once, garnished with chopped coriander/cilantro.

GRAINS, RICE AND PASTA

BEEF AND PORCINI RAGÙ
WITH PAPPARDELLE

Tender, slow-cooked beef and dried porcini combine to create a richly flavourful ragù, perfect for dinner parties. For easy entertaining, make the ragù a day or two in advance, cool and chill, allowing it to mature and mellow before reheating.

25 g/1 oz. dried porcini
3 tablespoons olive oil
600 g/1¼ lb. piece
    of beef silverside/
    bottom round
    or brisket
1 onion, finely chopped
1 celery stalk, finely
    chopped
½ carrot, finely chopped
2 sprigs of rosemary
1 bay leaf
dash of red or dry
    white wine
600 ml/2½ cups beef
    or chicken stock/
    broth
500 g/2 cups tomato
    passata/strained
    tomatoes
1 garlic clove
1 teaspoon porcini
    powder (cep powder)
250 g/8 oz. portobello
    mushrooms, roughly
    chopped
600 g/20 oz. fresh
    pappardelle pasta
salt and freshly ground
    black pepper
freshly grated
    Parmesan, to serve

SERVES 6

Preheat the oven to 150°C (300°F) Gas 2.

Soak the porcini in 200 ml/ 1 scant cup of boiling water for 20 minutes; strain to remove any grit, reserving the soaking water.

Heat 1 tablespoon olive oil in a large casserole dish. Add the beef, browning well on all sides. Remove and reserve.

Add another tablespoon olive oil to the casserole dish. Add the onion, celery, carrot, rosemary and bay leaf and fry, stirring often, for 5 minutes. Return the beef to the casserole. Pour over the wine and cook off over a high heat for 2 minutes. Add the porcini, the strained soaking water, stock/broth, passata/ strained tomatoes and garlic clove. Season with porcini powder, salt and pepper. Bring to the boil, cover and transfer to the preheated oven.

Cook for 1½ hours, until the beef is tender.

Remove the beef from the ragù and shred into small pieces. Return the shredded beef to the ragù. Cook, uncovered, over a medium heat for 30–40 minutes until reduced.

Heat the remaining olive oil in a separate frying pan/skillet. Fry the mushrooms for 2–3 minutes until lightly browned. Add the fried mushrooms to the beef ragù, mixing in. Simmer for 5 minutes.

Meanwhile, bring a large pan of salted water to the boil. Add the pappardelle and cook until just tender; drain.

Serve the pappardelle with the beef and porcini ragù and freshly grated Parmesan cheese.

FUNGI RISOTTO

When it comes to comfort food, a creamy-textured risotto is always a winner. This rice dish, flavoured with umami-rich dried porcini and succulent with fresh mushrooms, is deeply satisfying. For the best results, use good-quality chicken stock/broth. I've used portobello mushrooms, but you can use any combination of fresh mushrooms you wish.

25 g/1 oz. dried porcini
approx. 900 ml/4 cups
 good chicken stock/
 broth
40 g/2½ tablespoons
 butter
1 tablespoon olive oil
1 shallot, finely chopped
1 bay leaf
250 g/8 oz. portobello
 mushrooms, chopped
300 g/1½ cups Arborio
 risotto rice
25 ml/2 tablespoons
 dry white wine
freshly grated nutmeg
25 g/¼ cup grated
 Parmesan cheese,
 plus extra for serving
salt and freshly ground
 black pepper

SERVES 4

Soak the dried porcini in 300 ml/1¼ cups of warm water for 15 minutes; strain, reserving the water.

Place the stock in a pan, add the porcini soaking water and bring to a gentle simmer.

Heat 25 g/2 tablespoons butter and the olive oil in a large, heavy saucepan. Add the shallot and fry gently, stirring, until softened. Add the bay leaf and portobello mushrooms and fry, stirring often, for 2 minutes. Mix in the rice, coating well, and fry for 1 minute.

Add the white wine and cook off quickly over a medium heat, stirring. Mix in the porcini. Add in around 200 ml/1 scant cup simmering stock/broth and cook over a medium heat, stirring until absorbed. Add a further 100 ml/scant ½ cup and repeat the process until the rice is cooked through, but retains some bite.

Stir in the remaining butter and the Parmesan. Season with salt, pepper and nutmeg. Serve at once, with extra grated Parmesan on the side.

CREAMY MUSHROOM, RED PEPPER, AND BASIL PASTA SPIRALS

When it comes to speedy meals, where would we be without pasta? This recipe is perfect for a work-night meal – quick and easy to throw together, but delivering on flavour and texture. The 'meaty' bite of mushrooms works well here, giving the dish some body. Serve with a crisp green side salad.

1 red (bell) pepper
200 g/7 oz. pasta
    spirals
1 tablespoon olive oil
1 garlic clove,
    finely chopped
250 g/9 oz.
    mushrooms, sliced
    5-mm/¼-inch thick
a splash of dry white
    wine or Amontillado
    sherry
300 ml/1¼ cups
    double/heavy cream
2 tablespoons
    pine nuts, dry-fried
a generous handful
    of basil leaves,
    roughly torn
salt and freshly ground
    black pepper
freshly grated
    Parmesan cheese,
    to serve

SERVES 4

Preheat the grill/broiler to hot. Cook the red (bell) pepper under the hot grill/broiler, turning until charred all over. Remove, wrap in a plastic bag and set aside to cool. Once cool, peel and discard the charred skin, de-seed the pepper and cut into short chunky strips.

Bring a large pan of salted water to the boil. Add the pasta spirals and cook, following the package instructions, until al dente; drain.

Meanwhile, heat the olive oil in a large frying pan/skillet. Add the garlic and fry briefly until fragrant. Add the mushrooms and fry over a high heat, stirring often, for 5 minutes until lightly browned. Add the roasted red (bell) pepper strips and a splash of white wine. Cook briefly, mixing thoroughly, then add the cream, pine nuts and half the basil. Season with salt and pepper. Bring the cream to the boil, then reduce the heat and simmer gently for 3–5 minutes, stirring now and then.

Toss the cooked pasta spirals with the creamy mushroom sauce. Mix in the remaining basil. Serve at once, with freshly grated Parmesan.

GOCHUJANG-GLAZED MUSHROOM AND WHOLE GRAIN RICE BOWLS

There is something very appealing about bowl food. Here, classic Korean flavourings – including gochujang (Korean chilli paste), aromatic root ginger and pungent garlic – transform delicate, fresh exotic mushrooms into a piquant, flavourful topping for a bowl of rice.

300 g/1½ cups whole grain brown rice, rinsed

2 teaspoons gochujang (Korean chilli paste) or sweet chilli sauce

2 tablespoons rice wine or Amontillado sherry

2 tablespoons light soy sauce

2 teaspoons sugar (just 1 teaspoon if using sweet chilli sauce)

1 tablespoon vegetable oil

1 garlic clove, chopped

a thumb-sized piece of root ginger, chopped into fine strips

2 spring onions/scallions, white parts only, cut into short lengths

½ red (bell) pepper, deseeded and cut into strips

400 g/14 oz. assorted fresh oyster, shiitake, king oyster, shiro-shimeji mushrooms, any large ones sliced

50 g/⅔ cup mangetout/snowpeas, cut into short pieces

2 tablespoons raw cashew nuts

salt and freshly ground black pepper

handful of coriander/cilantro sprigs, to garnish

SERVES 4

Place the rice in a heavy-based saucepan. Add 400 ml/1⅔ cups of water and season with a pinch of salt. Bring to the boil, then reduce the heat, cover and simmer over a low heat for 25 minutes, until the rice is tender.

Five minutes before the rice is ready, mix together the gochujang, rice wine or sherry, soy sauce and sugar in a small bowl to form a paste.

Heat the oil in a wok or large frying pan/skillet over a medium-high heat. Add the garlic, ginger and spring onions/scallions. Fry, stirring, for 1 minute until fragrant. Add the red (bell) pepper, mushrooms, mangetout/snowpeas and cashews and stir-fry over a high heat for 2–3 minutes until the mushrooms are lightly browned. Add the gochujang paste mixture and stir in well to coat the ingredients. Stir-fry for 1–2 minutes until all the vegetables and mushrooms are glazed and sticky.

Divide the cooked and drained rice among four bowls and top each portion with some of the glazed mushrooms and veg. Garnish with coriander/cilantro and serve at once.

MUSHROOM MAC 'N' CHEESE

Served warm from the oven, a hearty dish of macaroni cheese is a perennial favourite. Here, the rich cheese sauce is flavoured with bay and mustard, and combined with a tasty mixture of fried leek, mushrooms and ham. A crunchy topping gives the finishing touch.

200 g/2 cups macaroni
   or short penne pasta
40 g/3 tablespoons
   butter
1 bay leaf
40 g/5 tablespoons
   plain/all-purpose
   flour
600 ml/2½ cups
   full fat/whole milk
125 g/1¼ cups
   Cheddar cheese,
   grated
1 teaspoon wholegrain
   mustard
freshly grated nutmeg
1 tablespoon sunflower
   oil
1 leek, finely chopped
200 g/6½ oz. button
   mushrooms, halved
100 g/3½ oz. pulled/
   shredded or diced
   cooked ham
2 tablespoons grated
   Parmesan cheese
25 g/⅓ cup fresh
   breadcrumbs
1 tablespoon pine nuts
salt and freshly ground
   black pepper
a shallow baking dish

SERVES 4

Preheat the oven to 200°C (400°F) Gas 6.

Bring a large pan of salted water to the boil. Add the pasta and cook, following the package instructions, until slightly underdone; drain.

Melt the butter with the bay leaf in a heavy-based saucepan. Mix in the flour and cook briefly, stirring. Gradually stir in the milk, mixing well with each addition. Cook, stirring, over a medium heat until the mixture thickens. Stir in the Cheddar cheese until melted. Stir in the mustard and season with nutmeg, salt and black pepper. Turn off the heat and set aside until needed.

Heat the oil in a frying pan/skillet over a low heat. Add the leek and fry gently for 5 minutes until softened, without allowing it to brown. Add the mushrooms, increase the heat, and fry briefly, stirring, until the mushrooms are lightly browned. Season with salt and freshly ground pepper.

In a large bowl, mix together the cooked macaroni pasta, the mushroom mixture and the pulled/shredded ham. Mix in the cheese sauce. Tip into the shallow baking dish. Sprinkle with the Parmesan cheese, breadcrumbs and pine nuts. Bake in the preheated oven for 30 minutes until golden brown on top. Serve at once.

MEET THE MUSHROOM GROWERS

Humans have cultivated mushrooms for centuries, as well as foraging for wild ones. France was an early pioneer, and in 1600 French agriculturalist Olivier de Serres first outlined a growing method. Mushrooms were cultivated in cool, damp cellars and caves and, in appropriate climates, grown outdoors on logs. Mushroom varieties that require a mycorrhizal relationship with the roots of a mature tree – such as ceps – have always proved the hardest to cultivate commercially. Progress in cultivation methods during the 20th century means that now a wide range of mushrooms are successfully grown around the world and seasonal wild mushrooms are grown throughout the year.

**Cynan Jones, The Mushroom Garden,
Glan Meirion, Wales, UK**
An imaginative project to encourage new, high-value crops in north Wales was the catalyst for Cynan

Jones to set up his mushroom-growing business in Snowdonia in 2005, specializing in shiitake and oyster mushrooms. 'It is a two-stage system' he explains. Sterilized wood chips are colonized with spawn (germinating mushroom spores) and placed in a warm environment to encourage the creation of the mycelium (the growing body of the fungus). The mycelium is then transferred to a cooler, more humid room (an environment which is 'similar to Wales all year round!' observes Cynan). This move mimics the arrival of autumn/fall and triggers the growth of mushrooms. The process of growing them is labour-intensive, with the mushrooms harvested morning and night. While some of his mushrooms are sold fresh, the majority are dried and sold whole, or turned into seasoning powders such as umami. 'Drying intensifies their flavour,' explains Cynan. 'We have a development kitchen. We love experimenting all the time with different flavours.'

Mushroom enthusiast and grower, Cynan Jones

Wild mushrooms

Jim Angelucci, Phillips Mushroom Farms, Kennett Square, Pennsylvania, USA

The state of Pennsylvania produces 68 per cent of all mushrooms grown in the USA. A leader in this field is Phillips Mushroom Farms, a family-run business, founded in 1927 by William W. Phillips in Kennett Square, the historic hub of America's mushroom farming world. In 1979, the company became the first in America to grow shiitake mushrooms, at that time a novelty in the USA. Today they produce a wide range of fresh mushrooms, from white button to maitake. They are the largest grower of speciality mushrooms in America, distributing over 35 million pounds annually. State-of-the-art growing techniques have been embraced by Phillips at their farms. 'We control every aspect of the environment in the growing rooms – the temperature, humidity and carbon dioxide levels are constantly monitored to ensure that the crop will reach its highest level of production,' explains General Manager Jim Angelucci. 'Every mushroom is handpicked and it's the only crop I know that has to be harvested every day. A mushroom doubles in size in 24 hours so it's imperative that they be picked when they reach the proper level of maturity.' He is proud of their innovative approach: 'Our philosophy here is, if you ain't the lead dog, the scenery never changes.'

Noel Arnold, Li-Sun Exotic Mushrooms, Mittagong, New South Wales, Australia

In 1987, a disused railway tunnel offered microbiologist Dr Noel Arnold a suitable environment in which to pursue his interest in commercial mushroom breeding. A pioneering figure in Australia's mushroom growing scene, Noel initially encountered customer resistance to his Swiss brown mushrooms and shiitake; 'I had trouble selling the brown ones as people used to white mushrooms thought they were dirty mushrooms,' he recalls. Attitudes have changed, however, which he attributes to the fact that Australians now have a much increased knowledge of Asian cooking. The conditions in the tunnel – around 16–18°C (60–64°F) and 85 per cent humidity – 'are similar to cool-climate forests in China, Taiwan, Korea and Japan, where these mushrooms grow on dead logs. So my philosophy is to grow varieties in the tunnel alongside each other.' As a scientist, Noel has enjoyed the research aspect of his work, involving experimentation in importing, trialling and selecting mushroom cultures, as well as finding suitable wood substrates. His strict attention to hygiene in the laboratory ensures he can grow mushrooms safely without the use of chemicals. His company, Li-Sun Exotic Mushrooms, now offers a range of nine mushrooms, including nameko, wood ear and enoki. When he first started, his sales were primarily to restaurants; now, he observes, 'the majority of sales are through the supermarkets.'

CHICKPEA AND MUSHROOM FREEKEH PILAF

With its subtle smoky flavour, freekeh (made from young durum wheat) is a great grain to cook with. Here, it is combined with nutty chickpeas and earthy mushrooms to make an appealing, colourful Middle Eastern pilaf. Serve as a meal on its own or as an accompaniment to grilled/broiled lamb or poultry, with yogurt on the side.

1 tablespoon butter

1 red onion, ½ chopped, ½ sliced

½ cinnamon stick

3 cardamom pods

½ tablespoon coriander seeds

250 g/1¼ cups freekeh (roasted green durum wheat), rinsed

400 ml/1⅔ cups chicken or vegetable stock/broth

1 tablespoon olive oil

1 garlic clove, chopped

250 g/8 oz. white/cup mushrooms, sliced 1-cm/⅜-inch thick

1 x 400-g/14-oz. can of chickpeas in water, drained

salt

4 tablespoons pomegranate seeds, to garnish

freshly chopped coriander/cilantro, to garnish

SERVES 4

Heat the butter in a heavy-based saucepan. Add the chopped red onion, cinnamon stick, cardamom and coriander seeds and fry, stirring a little, over a gentle heat for 2–3 minutes.

Add the freekeh, mixing well to coat in the flavoured butter. Add the stock/broth and season with salt. Bring to the boil. Cover, reduce the heat and simmer for 20–25 minutes over a very low heat until the stock/broth has reduced and the freekeh grains have softened.

Heat the olive oil in a frying pan/skillet. Fry the sliced red onion and garlic over a medium heat for 2 minutes, until softened and fragrant. Add the mushrooms and fry over a high heat, stirring, until lightly browned.

Fold two-thirds of the chickpeas into the freekeh. Place the mixture in a serving dish. Top with the freshly fried mushrooms and remaining chickpeas. Sprinkle with the pomegranate seeds and coriander/cilantro to garnish. Serve at once.

400 g/12 oz. assorted
mushrooms (half
cultivated, half wild)
200 g/1⅓ cups
instant polenta
2 tablespoons butter
1 tablespoon olive oil
½ red onion, sliced
1 garlic clove, chopped
1 sprig of fresh
rosemary
salt and freshly ground
black pepper
freshly chopped
parsley, to garnish
grated Parmesan
cheese, to serve

SERVES 4

POLENTA WITH WILD MUSHROOMS

Comfort food, Italian-style! This dish features sautéed wild and cultivated mushrooms on a bed of polenta. Simple but *delizioso*!

Cut the cultivated mushrooms into 1-cm/³/₈-inch-thick slices. Trim the wild mushrooms.

Bring 2 litres/quarts of generously salted water to the boil in a large saucepan. Add the polenta in a steady stream, stirring vigorously with a wooden spoon as you do so in order to prevent lumps forming. Cook, stirring, until the mixture thickens, a matter of around 5 minutes. Mix in the butter and keep warm over a low heat.

Heat the olive oil in a large, heavy frying pan/skillet. Add the red onion, garlic and rosemary and fry for 2 minutes, until the onion has softened. Add the wild and cultivated mushrooms and fry over a high heat for 3–4 minutes, until browned and just softened. Season with salt and freshly ground black pepper. Discard the rosemary sprig.

Serve the warm polenta topped with the mushroom mixture and plenty of extra ground black pepper. Garnish with chopped parsley, and serve with grated Parmesan cheese on the side.

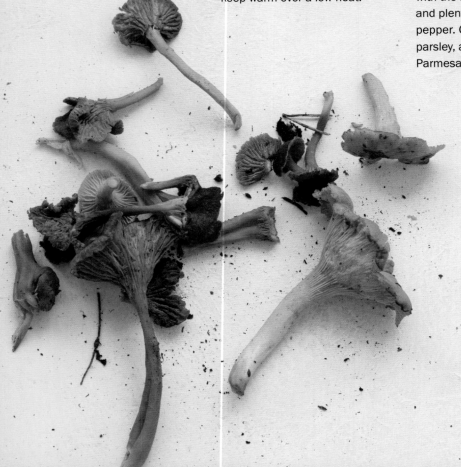

TRUFFLED MUSHROOM LASAGNE

15 g/½ oz. dried porcini
2 tablespoons olive oil
1 onion, finely chopped
1 celery stalk, finely
  chopped
½ carrot, peeled and
  finely chopped
2 fresh sage leaves,
  shredded
1 rosemary sprig, leaves
  finely chopped
200 g/6½ oz. white/
  cup mushrooms,
  finely chopped
500 g/1 lb. minced/
  ground beef
1 garlic clove, finely
  chopped
100 ml/scant ½ cup
  red wine
500 g/2 cups passata/
  strained tomatoes
200 ml/1 scant cup
  beef stock/broth
50 g/3 tablespoons
  butter
6 tablespoons plain/
  all-purpose flour
600 ml/2½ cups milk
3 tablespoons double/
  heavy cream
1 teaspoon truffle oil
9–12 dried lasagne
  sheets
50 g/⅔ cup grated
  Parmesan cheese
salt and freshly ground
  black pepper

SERVES 6

A rich, sophisticated take on lasagne. Ideal for entertaining as it can be made in advance; serve it simply with an elegant fennel and rocket/arugula salad on the side.

Soak the dried porcini in hot water for 20 minutes; drain and chop.

To make the meat sauce, heat the olive oil in a casserole dish or Dutch oven over a medium heat. Add the onion, celery, carrot, sage and rosemary and fry, stirring, for 2–3 minutes, until the onion has softened. Then add the porcini and white/cup mushrooms and cook, stirring, for 2 minutes.

Add the beef and fry until browned on all sides, stirring to mix with the mushrooms. Sprinkle in the garlic and add the red wine. Cook, stirring, for 2–3 minutes until the red wine has largely reduced. Add the passata/strained tomatoes and beef stock/broth. Season with salt and freshly ground black pepper. Bring to the boil, then lower the heat and simmer uncovered for 1 hour, stirring occasionally, until the sauce is thickened and reduced.

Meanwhile, make the white sauce. Melt the butter in

a heavy-based saucepan. Add the flour and cook, stirring, for 2 minutes. Gradually add the milk, stirring well with each addition to ensure that there are no lumps. Season with salt and freshly ground black pepper. Bring to the boil, while stirring, until the sauce thickens. Stir in the cream and the truffle oil. Set aside.

Preheat the oven to 200°C (400°F) Gas 6.

In a baking dish, place a spoonful of the meat sauce, spreading it thinly over the base. Add a layer of lasagne sheets. Top with another layer of the meat sauce, then spread 1–2 tablespoons of the truffled white sauce over the meat. Sprinkle with a little Parmesan. Repeat the layering process, finishing with a generous layer of the white sauce and topping with the remaining Parmesan.

Bake the lasagne in the preheated oven for 40 minutes, until golden-brown. Serve straight away.

HAZELNUT, MUSHROOM
AND BULGUR WHEAT SALAD

Finely sliced mushrooms are a great addition to salads, adding a fresh, clean flavour and distinctive, delicate texture. Here they are combined to good effect with dry-fried hazelnuts, juicy tomatoes, bulgur wheat and a tangy pomegranate molasses dressing to make a vibrant, colourful salad, inspired by the flavours of the Middle East. Serve this as a side-dish with grilled/broiled meat or the Mushroom and Halloumi Kebabs (page 143), or as part of a mezze feast.

100 g/½ cup bulgur wheat
100 g/⅔ cup blanched hazelnuts
100 g/¾ cup cherry tomatoes, quartered
½ red (bell) pepper, deseeded and diced
1 spring onion/scallion, finely chopped
3 tablespoons extra virgin olive oil

3 tablespoons pomegranate molasses
50 g/1 small bunch fresh parsley, very finely chopped
150 g/5 oz. white/cup mushrooms, thinly sliced
salt and freshly ground black pepper

SERVES 4

Soak the bulgur wheat in boiling water for 5 minutes to soften; drain.

Dry-fry the hazelnuts in a frying pan/skillet for 2–3 minutes until golden-brown, stirring often. Leave to cool and then finely chop.

In a large bowl, mix together the bulgur wheat, toasted hazelnuts, cherry tomatoes, red (bell) pepper and spring onion/scallion. Add the extra virgin olive oil and pomegranate molasses. Season well with salt and freshly ground black pepper, and mix thoroughly. Mix in the parsley, then the mushrooms. Serve at once.

MEAT, POULTRY AND FISH

UMAMI STEAKS WITH WILD MUSHROOMS

This simple but luxurious dish is a great way to enjoy wild mushrooms.

4 sirloin steaks, each approx. 150 g/5 oz.
   and 2-cm/¾-inch thick,
   at room temperature
2 tablespoons olive oil
4 tablespoons ground dried porcini
   (cep powder)
200 g/6½ oz. assorted wild mushrooms,
   such as chanterelles and porcini,
   or assorted cultivated mushrooms
salt and freshly ground black pepper
2 griddle pans/ridged stovetop grill pans

SERVES 4

Coat all the steaks thoroughly in 1 tablespoon of the olive oil, then coat well in the dried porcini powder on both sides. Season with salt and freshly ground black pepper.

Trim the wild mushrooms. If using cultivated mushrooms, cut them into ½-cm/³⁄₁₆-inch-thick slices.

Heat the griddle pans/ridged stovetop grill pans until very hot. Cook the steaks on the pans to your taste, turning over during the process. For medium-rare, allow around 2 minutes on each side.

Meanwhile, heat a heavy-based frying pan/skillet until hot. Add the remaining olive oil and heat through. Fry the wild mushrooms briefly over a high heat, until just browned and slightly softened. Season with salt and freshly ground black pepper. Serve each steak topped with a portion of the sautéed wild mushrooms.

TRUFFLED FRIES

Freshly cooked fries flavoured with truffle oil are a decadent treat. Serve with drinks as an appetizing snack or as a side-dish with grilled/broiled fish, hamburgers or the Umami Steaks (left).

500 g/1 lb. Maris Piper or Russet Burbank
   potatoes
sunflower or vegetable oil, for deep-frying
sea salt
½ teaspoon truffle oil
kitchen thermometer

SERVES 4 AS A SNACK
OR 2 AS A SIDE

Peel and cut the potatoes into 1-cm/³⁄₈-inch-thick strips. Rinse briefly to wash off the excess starch, then thoroughly pat dry with a clean kitchen cloth.

Pour the sunflower or vegetable oil into a deep, heavy-based saucepan so that it reaches a third of the way up the sides. Preheat the oil to 120°C (250°F). Cooking in batches, add a handful of the potato strips to the oil and fry for 4 minutes, until softened but not browned. Remove with a slotted spoon and drain on paper towels. Repeat the process until all the potatoes have been fried.

Increase the temperature of the oil in the pan to 180°C (350°F). Again, frying in batches, return the chips to the oil and fry for a few minutes until they turn deep gold in colour. Remove and drain on paper towels.

Once all the chips have been fried twice, sprinkle with sea salt and truffle oil, tossing well to spread thoroughly. Serve at once.

YAKITORI-GLAZED MUSHROOM AND CHICKEN SKEWERS

These salty-sweet glazed chicken skewers go down well with all the family! Fresh shiitake mushrooms, with their distinctive flavour, are a pleasing element in the dish. Serve simply with jasmine rice or sushi rice and blanched pak choi/bok choy, gai laan or spinach.

16 white/cup mushrooms, stalks trimmed off
250 g/8 oz. boneless chicken breast, cut into short, thin strips
16 fresh shiitake mushrooms, halved, stalks trimmed off
½ green (bell) pepper, deseeded and cut into 2- x 2-cm/³⁄₄- x ³⁄₄-inch squares
2 spring onions/scallions, cut into 2-cm/³⁄₄-inch lengths
finely chopped red chilli/chile, to garnish (optional)

YAKITORI GLAZE
50 ml/3 tablespoons rice wine or Amontillado sherry
50 ml/3 tablespoons mirin
50 ml/3 tablespoons light soy sauce
1 tablespoon white granulated sugar
¼ teaspoon salt
8 metal or soaked wooden cooking skewers

SERVES 4

Make the yakitori glaze by placing the rice wine or sherry, mirin, soy sauce, sugar and salt in a small saucepan. Bring to the boil and boil for 1 minute until melted together into a syrupy glaze. Turn off the heat.

Thread the white/cup mushrooms, chicken, shiitake mushrooms, green (bell) pepper and spring onions/scallions onto the 8 skewers.

TRUFFLED ROAST CHICKEN

Roast chicken will always be a favourite. In this recipe, this much-loved classic takes on a sophisticated edge with the addition of a flavourful mushroom stuffing and a truffle-flavoured butter inserted under the skin to ensure gloriously succulent, tasty results. Serve with mashed potatoes and an array of side-vegetables such as cauliflower or broccoli, green beans and carrots.

1 tablespoon olive oil
½ onion, finely chopped
200 g/6½ oz.
   chestnut/cremini
   mushrooms, chopped
25 g/1 oz. assorted
   dried mushrooms
   (girolles, morels,
   black trumpets,
   porcini), soaked
   in hot water for
   25 minutes, drained
   and chopped
25 g/⅓ cup fresh
   breadcrumbs
2 teaspoons truffle oil
50 g/3 tablespoons
   butter, softened
1 teaspoon dried porcini
   powder (cep powder)
1 x 2 kg/4½ lb. chicken
salt and freshly ground
   black pepper

SERVES 4

Preheat the oven to 200°C (400°F) Gas 6.

First, prepare the stuffing. Heat the olive oil in a frying pan/skillet over a medium heat. Add the onion and fry until softened. Add the mushrooms and fry, stirring, until lightly browned. Remove from the heat and mix together with the dried mushrooms, breadcrumbs and 1 teaspoon of the truffle oil. Season with salt and freshly ground black pepper. Set aside.

In a small bowl, mash together the butter, dried porcini powder and remaining truffle oil.

Season the chicken skin with salt and freshly ground black pepper.

Loosen the skin on the chicken breasts and insert a layer of the butter mixture between the skin and the flesh on both sides. Fill the chicken cavity with the mushroom stuffing mixture.

Roast the chicken in the preheated oven for 1 hour 50 minutes, basting often with the buttery juices, until cooked through. Set the chicken aside to rest in a warm place for 20 minutes, before carving and serving with a gravy made from the roasting juices, if desired.

PAN-FRIED FISH FILLETS WITH WILD MUSHROOMS

The delicate flavours of wild mushrooms work well with light-textured white fish, making this a great, quickly-cooked dinner party dish.

200 g/6½ oz. assorted wild mushrooms or assorted cultivated mushrooms
3 tablespoons olive oil
30 g/2 tablespoons butter
4 white fish fillets, skin on, each approx. 175 g/6 oz.
1 shallot, chopped
1 bay leaf
1 tablespoon dry white wine
squeeze of fresh lemon juice
grated zest of ½ lemon
1 tablespoon freshly chopped parsley
salt and freshly ground black pepper

SERVES 4

Carefully trim the wild mushrooms. If using cultivated mushrooms, cut into ½-cm/³⁄₁₆-inch-thick slices.

Heat a large heavy frying pan/skillet until hot. Add 2 tablespoons of the olive oil and the butter and heat through. Add the fish fillets, skin-side down, and fry over a medium-high heat for around 3 minutes, until the skin has coloured and crisped. Carefully, turn over and fry for a further 2–3 minutes, or until the flesh has turned opaque and the fish is cooked through. Season with salt and freshly ground black pepper.

Meanwhile, heat the remaining olive oil in a separate frying pan/skillet. Fry the shallot and bay leaf gently until the shallot has softened. Add the wild mushrooms and fry, stirring gently to coat well with the oil, over a high heat for 2 minutes. Add the white wine and cook for 1 minute. Add the lemon juice, zest and parsley. Season with salt and freshly ground black pepper.

Serve the fish fillets with the wild mushrooms on the side.

BEEF AND MUSHROOM STROGANOFF

Succulent steak strips, fried with plump mushrooms and shallot, then cooked with brandy and enriched with a sour cream sauce – stroganoff is a classic dish for good reason. While, gloriously, it can be cooked in minutes, it also delivers a wonderful depth of flavour. Serve with steamed rice and a side-vegetable, such as broccoli or cabbage.

2 tablespoons olive oil
300 g/10 oz. chestnut/
    cremini mushrooms,
    cut into 1-cm/
    ³/₈-inch slices
1 banana shallot,
    sliced lengthways
1 bay leaf
500 g/1 lb. rump steak,
    cut into short,
    thin strips
1 teaspoon paprika
3 tablespoons brandy
300 ml/1¼ cups sour
    cream
2 teaspoons wholegrain
    mustard
salt and freshly ground
    black pepper
freshly chopped parsley,
    to garnish

SERVES 4

Heat 1 tablespoon of the olive oil in a large frying pan/skillet over a medium heat. Add the mushrooms and fry quickly until lightly browned; remove from pan and reserve.

Add the remaining oil to the pan. Add the shallot and bay leaf and fry over a low–medium heat until softened. Increase the heat to medium, add the steak and fry until lightly browned. Return the mushrooms to the pan.

Add the paprika, mixing it in well. Pour over the brandy and cook over a high heat for 2–3 minutes to cook off the alcohol. Reduce the heat to medium, add the sour cream and mustard and then season with salt and freshly ground black pepper. Cook briefly, for about 3 minutes, until the sauce is heated through, stirring well. Garnish with chopped parsley and serve at once.

BEEF WELLINGTON

75 g/⅔ cup plain/
   all-purpose flour
a pinch of salt
1 teaspoon dried porcini
   (cep powder),
   optional
3 eggs
100 ml/⅓ cup plus
   1 tablespoon milk
butter, for frying the
   pancakes
2 tablespoons olive oil
1 banana shallot,
   finely chopped
250 g/8 oz. field
   mushrooms,
   finely chopped
250 g/8 oz. chestnut/
   cremini mushrooms,
   finely chopped
15 g/½ oz. dried
   porcini, soaked in hot
   water for 20 minutes,
   then squeezed dry,
   chopped
freshly grated nutmeg
700 g/1½ lb. piece of
   beef fillet of even
   thickness
1 tablespoon Dijon or
   wholegrain mustard
300 g/10 oz. ready-
   made puff pastry
salt and freshly ground
   black pepper
beaten egg, to glaze
25-cm/10-inch frying
   pan/skilllet

SERVES 6

This dinner party classic requires a fair bit of preparation. However, it looks splendid and tastes wonderful.

Sift the flour into a mixing bowl. Stir in the salt and the dried porcini powder (if using). Break the eggs into the centre, then gradually whisk in the milk to form a smooth pancake batter.

Heat a small knob/pat of butter in the 25-cm/10-inch frying pan/skillet over a medium heat. When the butter is foaming, pour in a quarter of the pancake batter, tilting the pan to spread it evenly. Fry the pancake until set, then flip over to lightly brown on the other side. Remove from the pan. Repeat to make four pancakes in total. Leave to cool.

Heat 1 tablespoon of olive oil in a large, heavy frying pan/skillet. Add the shallot and fry gently over a low heat for 3 minutes, stirring, until softened. Add the chopped mushrooms. Season with salt, pepper and nutmeg. Fry, stirring, for 20 minutes until the mixture is dry. Turn into a colander. Leave to cool, then cover and chill for 1 hour.

Season the beef with salt and pepper. Heat the remaining oil in a large frying pan/skillet over a high heat. Add the beef and brown on all sides. Set aside to cool, wrap and chill for 1 hour.

To assemble, place a large rectangle of cling film/plastic wrap on a work surface. Place the four pancakes on top and overlap the edges to form a rough 'rectangle', large enough to encase the beef. Spread the mushroom mixture over the pancakes. Brush the beef with the mustard. Place the beef in the centre of the pancakes and use the plastic wrap to roll into a parcel, tucking in the corners. Twist the plastic ends together tightly and chill for 30 minutes.

Roll out the pastry to form two large rectangles, one larger than the other. Unwrap the chilled beef and place in the centre of the smaller rectangle. Brush the edges of the pastry with beaten egg. Place the second rectangle over the beef, pressing the edges together and patterning with a fork. Trim to form a neat parcel. Chill for 30 minutes.

Preheat the oven to 200°C (400°F) Gas 6. Place the wellington on a baking sheet and thoroughly brush with beaten egg. Bake in the preheated oven for 40 minutes until golden-brown. Stand for 10 minutes before serving in thick slices.

Field mushrooms (*Agaricus campestris*)

Wild mushrooms for sale

WILD MUSHROOMS

Long before humans began cultivating mushrooms, we sought out wild mushrooms with which to enhance our diet. In certain countries, foraging for fungi has been a popular pastime for generations. These seasonal foods which have to be searched for have a particular prize-like allure. In Japan, the rare matsutake mushroom, which grows near pine trees, is a highly sought-after luxury, commanding high prices. Truffles, of course, are another example.

In France, Italy, Poland and Russia, hunting for mushrooms is almost a national obsession. At certain times of the year (most often the autumn/fall) mushroom enthusiasts in these countries head out into the countryside equipped with small, sharp knives and baskets to see what they can find. Finding mushrooms for free, that would otherwise cost a lot, is certainly part of the appeal. Really fresh mushrooms also have the best flavour, so being able to cook and eat just-picked wild mushrooms is a very special treat.

Gathering and consuming wild mushrooms, however, entails a risk factor. A number of species will cause illnesses – such as an upset stomach or vomiting – while a few species are so toxic that they can be fatal. For the would-be mushroom forager it is essential to be absolutely sure that the mushroom picked is safe to eat. Buying a good, detailed, illustrated guide is a starting point. In France and Italy, pharmacies offer an identification service to ensure that the foraged fungi are safe to eat. In countries, such as Britain, however, which lack a mushroom-hunting culture, this service is not provided, so extra care and attention is required. If, having eaten wild mushrooms, you develop any strange symptoms, it's important to immediately seek medical attention at a hospital.

The best way to learn the dos and don'ts of mushroom-picking is to go out with a knowledgeable mushroom enthusiast. Nowadays in the UK, it is possible to take part in guided walks to find and

Brick tuft mushrooms
(*Hypholoma sublateritium*) grow
in clusters on tree stumps

Highly prized Chanterelles (*Cantharellus cibarius*)

identify fungi. Going on a mushroom-identification walk on London's Hampstead Heath with expert Andy Overall, founder of Fungi To Be With, proved to be a really interesting experience. To begin with, the expedition brought home to me what a huge variety of colours, shapes and sizes fungi come in – not just the familiar 'umbrella' mushroom shapes we know from the supermarket. Particularly striking examples were a huge slab of scarlet beefsteak mushroom, clusters of hen of the woods mushrooms and dense, inedible birch bracket, growing shelf-like on tree trunks. The names were noticeably descriptive: sulphur tuft, bleeding mycena, poison pie, ink cap... Old wood, we learned, is a good place for wild

mushrooms to grow on, so fallen tree trunks and stumps were looked at with a new interest. What was evident, however, was how few of the fungi we found could be eaten. In Britain, of the 3,000 larger fungi, only around 100 are edible. As members of the group showed Andy their finds, 'inedible' and 'toxic' were the words used most frequently! What also struck me, was the potential for confusion from dangerous look-alikes. Bright yellow mushrooms turned out to be 'false chanterelles', only recognizable to Andy's experienced eye because their gills are 'more pronounced' than those of true chanterelles. It turns out there are several aspects one needs to take into account when identifying wild mushrooms: such as the size, colour and texture of the cap and stem; the colour and shape of the gills; the texture of the flesh and the mushroom's habitat. The fact that there is so much to learn is precisely why Andy has become so fascinated by wild mushrooms; the complex world of fungi certainly has the capacity to enthral. As humans, we enjoy the primal satisfaction of hunter-gathering and – despite the risks – the appeal of hunting for wild mushrooms endures.

STIR-FRIED BEEF WITH MUSHROOMS

A key flavouring in Chinese cuisine, dried shiitake mushrooms give a wonderful depth of flavour to a variety of dishes. Here, they are combined with tender strips of beef and white/cup mushrooms in a quickly-cooked stir-fry, flavoured with garlic and spring onions/scallions. Serve with jasmine rice or egg noodles for an easy meal.

6 dried shiitake
    mushrooms
2 tablespoons rice wine
    or sherry
4 tablespoons light
    soy sauce
350 g/12 oz. beef,
    cut into thin strips
1 tablespoon olive oil
1 garlic clove,
    finely chopped
4 spring onions/
    scallions, chopped
    into 2.5-cm/1-inch
    lengths (whites and
    greens separated)
200 g/6½ oz. white/
    cup mushrooms,
    sliced 1-cm/⅜-inch
    thick
2 tablespoons oyster
    sauce
2 tablespoons chicken
    stock/broth
sliced fresh red chilli/
    chile, to garnish
    (optional)

SERVES 4

Pour boiling water over the dried shiitake mushrooms and set aside for 30 minutes to soak. Drain, then trim and discard the stalks and finely slice the softened shiitake.

In a medium bowl, mix together 1 tablespoon of the rice wine or sherry with 2 tablespoons of the soy sauce. Add the beef strips and set aside in the fridge to marinate for 30 minutes.

Heat a wok until very hot. Add the oil and heat through. Add the garlic and the white spring onions/scallions and stir-fry briefly until fragrant. Add the marinated beef and shiitake mushrooms and stir-fry for 2 minutes over high heat.

Add the white/cup mushroom slices, mixing in. Pour over the remaining 1 tablespoon of rice wine or sherry and allow to sizzle for 1 minute. Add the remaining 2 tablespoons of soy sauce, the oyster sauce and chicken stock/broth and stir-fry for 1–2 minutes. Sprinkle with the green spring onions/scallions and garnish with fresh chilli/chile, if desired. Serve at once.

PORK CHOPS WITH MUSHROOM AND APPLE CIDER SAUCE

A flavourful sauce transforms simple pork chops into a luxurious dish. Serve with mashed potatoes and green beans.

2 tablespoons olive oil
4 even-sized pork chops,
    each approx. 200 g/6½ oz.
1 tablespoon butter
1 onion, halved and sliced
1 dessert apple, cored and thinly sliced
100 g/3½ oz. button, dried shiitake and enoki
    mushrooms, cut into 1-cm/³/₈-inch slices
100 ml/scant ½ cup dry/hard cider
150 ml/²/₃ cup crème fraîche (or sour cream)
2 teaspoons wholegrain mustard
salt and freshly ground black pepper

SERVES 4

Heat 1 tablespoon of the olive oil in a large frying pan/skillet. Add the pork chops, seasoning with salt and black pepper. Fry over a medium heat for 12–15 minutes, turning halfway through, until golden-brown on both sides and cooked through.

Meanwhile, in a separate frying pan/skillet, heat the butter and remaining 1 tablespoon olive oil until frothing. Add the onion and fry until golden-brown. Add the apple and fry, stirring, for 2–3 minutes until lightly browned. Add the mushrooms and fry until lightly browned. Pour over the cider and simmer until reduced by half, stirring often. Stir in the crème fraîche and mustard. Season with salt and freshly ground pepper. Serve the warm pork chops with the mushroom and apple cider sauce.

ROAST MUSHROOM AND SAUSAGE TRAY BAKE

The perfect dish to make after a busy day, this tray bake is a pleasure to cook – all one has to do is mix the ingredients then bake together in the oven.

1 onion, roughly chopped
1 red (bell) pepper, deseeded and cut into
    broad strips
1 courgette/zucchini, chopped into 2.5-cm/
    1-inch chunks
250 g/8 oz. large white/cup mushrooms,
    trimmed
8 good-quality sausages
8 cherry tomatoes
2 thyme sprigs, leaves only
4 fresh sage leaves, roughly torn
2 tablespoons olive oil
salt and freshly ground black pepper

SERVES 4

Preheat the oven to 200°C (400°F) Gas 6.

In a large roasting tray, mix together the vegetables, mushrooms, sausages and herbs. Pour over the olive oil and mix well, coating evenly. Season with salt and freshly ground black pepper.

Roast in the preheated oven for 30–40 minutes until the sausages are cooked through, tossing once or twice during roasting to ensure even browning. Serve at once.

CHICKEN AND MUSHROOM PIE

Splendid to look at, with its creamy-textured sauce and satisfying filling, this is soothing comfort food in pie form! Serve it for Sunday lunch or as a dinner party centrepiece, accompanied by boiled new potatoes, broccoli and glazed carrots.

25 g/2 tablespoons butter
1 onion, finely chopped
25 g/3 tablespoons plain/all-purpose flour
400 ml/1²/₃ cups chicken stock/broth
2 tablespoons double/heavy cream
25 g/4–5 sprigs fresh parsley, finely chopped
1 tablespoon olive oil
300 g/10 oz. button mushrooms, halved
700 g/25 oz. cooked chicken, chopped into large chunks
150 g/1 cup cooked peas
250 g/8 oz. shortcrust pastry/pie crust dough
beaten egg, to glaze
salt and freshly ground black pepper
a 1.6-litre/9-inch circular pie dish/pan

SERVES 6

To make the sauce, melt the butter in a heavy-based saucepan. Add the onion and cook over a low–medium heat until softened, but not coloured. Mix in the flour and cook, stirring, for a minute. Gradually, add the stock, stirring as you do so to avoid lumps. Bring to the boil, stirring often, until thickened. Mix in the double/heavy cream and parsley. Season with salt and freshly ground black pepper. Set aside.

Heat the olive oil in a large frying pan/skillet. Fry the mushrooms over a medium heat until lightly browned. Set aside.

In the pie dish/pan, mix together the cooked chicken, peas and mushrooms. Stir through the sauce and set aside to cool.

Preheat the oven to 200°C (400°F) Gas 6.

Roll out the pastry thinly on a lightly floured surface. Cover the pie mixture with the pastry lid, using the pastry trimmings to decorate it to your liking. Cut 3 slashes or a hole in the crust to let steam escape. Brush the pastry with beaten egg. Bake in the preheated oven for 1 hour until the pastry is golden-brown. Serve hot from the oven.

SEAFOOD AND OYSTER MUSHROOM STIR-FRY

The delicate flavours of seafood and mushrooms go together a treat. Serve with jasmine rice or Chinese egg noodles for a speedy lunch or supper.

1 tablespoon vegetable oil
2.5-cm/1-inch piece of root ginger, shredded
1 leek, thinly sliced
200 g/6½ oz. peeled raw prawns/shrimp
200 g/6½ oz. small/bay scallops
150 g/5 oz. fresh shiitake mushrooms, sliced 1-cm/⅜-inch thick
150 g/5 oz. fresh oyster mushrooms
1 tablespoon rice wine or Amontillado sherry
1 tablespoon oyster sauce
1 teaspoon light soy sauce

SERVES 2

Heat a wok until very hot. Add the oil and heat through. Add the ginger and leek and stir-fry until fragrant. Add the prawns/shrimps, scallops and shiitake and oyster mushrooms. Stir-fry for 2–3 minutes until the seafood turns opaque.

Add the rice wine or sherry and cook off over high heat for 1–2 minutes, stirring. Add the oyster sauce and soy sauce. Stir-fry briefly. Serve at once.

SEA BASS FILLETS WITH SHIITAKE MUSHROOMS

In this elegant dish, both dried and fresh shiitake mushrooms add a depth of flavour to steamed sea bass fillets.

4 dried shiitake mushrooms
2 sea bass fillets, each 150 g/5 oz.
a pinch of sugar
2.5-cm/1-inch piece of root ginger, shredded
1 spring onion/scallion, shredded
4 fresh shiitake mushrooms, thinly sliced
2 tablespoons sunflower oil
1 tablespoon light soy sauce
salt and freshly ground black pepper
thinly sliced fresh red chilli/chile (optional)
a large lidded wok
a trivet
a lightly oiled, large-rimmed, heatproof dish

SERVES 2

Pour boiling water over the dried shiitake and set aside to soften for 30 minutes. Drain, trim, discard the stems and finely shred the shiitake.

Place the wok on the stovetop and put the trivet in the centre of the wok. Pour in boiling water to surround the trivet, so that it comes up half-way. Place the sea bass fillets on the oiled heatproof dish, sprinkle with the shredded dried shiitake, and balance the dish on the trivet. Cover the wok and steam the sea bass for 15 minutes, until the flesh is opaque and the fish cooked through.

Season the sea bass with salt and pepper and sugar. Sprinkle the ginger, spring onion/scallion and fresh shiitake evenly over the fillets. In a small frying pan/skillet, heat the oil until smoking hot. Pour the hot oil over the sea bass fillets, then the soy sauce. Serve at once, garnished with fresh chilli/chile, if desired.

TRUFFLED MASH COTTAGE PIE

Cottage pie goes upmarket! Using a touch of truffle oil to flavour the mashed potato is a simple but effective way to give a new dimension to this homely dish. Adding mushrooms to the meat mixture brings texture as well as flavour. Bake until golden-brown and serve it straight from the oven, accompanied by peas, beans or broccoli, for a satisfying meal.

1 tablespoon vegetable oil
1 bay leaf
1 onion, finely chopped
1 celery stalk, finely chopped
½ carrot, peeled and finely chopped
500 g/1 lb. lean minced/ground beef
150 g/5 oz. white/cup and button mushrooms, chopped
a splash of dry white wine (optional)
3 tablespoons tomato paste
100 ml/scant ½ cup beef or chicken stock/broth
900 g/2 lb. fluffy/Idaho potatoes, peeled and cut into chunks
2 teaspoons butter
2 tablespoons double/ heavy cream
½ teaspoon truffle oil
3 tablespoons grated Cheddar cheese
1 tablespoon grated Parmesan cheese
salt and freshly ground black pepper

SERVES 4

Preheat oven to 200°C (400°F) Gas 6.

Heat the oil in a large frying pan/skillet over a medium heat. Add in the bay leaf, onion, celery and carrot and fry, stirring, until the onion is softened. Add the minced/ground beef and fry until browned, stirring often.

Add the mushrooms and fry for 3 minutes. Pour in the white wine (if using) and fry briefly until cooked off. Mix in the tomato paste and the stock/broth. Season with salt and freshly ground black pepper. Simmer for 10–15 minutes, stirring often.

Meanwhile, cook the potatoes in a large pan of salted, boiling water until tender; drain. Mash with butter, cream and truffle oil and season with salt and freshly ground black pepper.

Place the beef mixture in an ovenproof dish. Top with the mashed potato, spreading in an even layer. Sprinkle over the Cheddar and Parmesan cheese.

Bake in the preheated oven for 30 minutes until golden-brown. Serve hot from the oven.

SALADS AND
VEGETABLE DISHES

MUSHROOM, FIG, SPINACH AND FETA SALAD

With their distinctive and delicate flavour, adding raw mushrooms to a dish is a delicious way of using them in the kitchen. Here earthy-tasting mushrooms are combined with salty feta cheese, crunchy fried walnuts and sweet-fleshed figs to create a quick-to-make, colourful and interesting salad, ideal for summer eating.

2½ tablespoons olive oil
50 g/⅓ cup walnut halves
1 tablespoon balsamic vinegar
200 g/6½ oz. baby spinach
100 g/3½ oz. feta cheese
200 g/6½ oz. white/cup mushrooms, thinly sliced
4 fresh figs, thinly sliced
salt and freshly ground black pepper

SERVES 4

Heat ½ tablespoon of the olive oil in a frying pan/skillet. Add the walnuts and fry over a medium heat, stirring often, until lightly browned. Set aside to cool.

Make a dressing by mixing together the remaining olive oil and balsamic vinegar. Season well with salt and freshly ground black pepper.

In a serving bowl, toss the spinach with the dressing. Crumble in the feta cheese and add in the walnuts, tossing to mix through. Top with the mushrooms and figs and serve at once.

CRAB, MUSHROOM AND FENNEL SALAD

Fresh crab is always a treat. This delightful, fresh-tasting salad is very easy to make, while the results are enticing and sophisticated. A perfect dinner party appetizer.

2 tablespoons extra-virgin olive oil
juice of ½ lemon
1 large fennel bulb, very thinly sliced,
   fronds reserved
200 g/6½ oz. white/cup mushrooms, thinly sliced
250 g/8 oz. fresh white crab meat
2 tomatoes, blanched, de-seeded and diced
grated zest of 1 lemon
2 tablespoons freshly chopped dill
salt and freshly ground black pepper

SERVES 4

Place the extra-virgin olive oil and lemon juice in a small clean jar and shake to mix together. Season with salt and pepper and shake again.

Gently mix together the fennel and mushrooms. Add the lemon oil dressing and carefully mix through. Place the fennel mixture in a salad serving dish. Top with crab meat and diced tomato. Sprinkle with the lemon zest and dill. Garnish with the reserved fennel fronds and serve at once.

MUSHROOM, CANNELLINI BEAN AND TUNA SALAD

The rustic flavours of beans and mushrooms go very well together, given a savoury kick by a zingy anchovy, mustard and lemon juice dressing. Serve for a light lunch or supper, with toasted rustic bread on the side.

200 g/1 cup of dried
    cannellini beans or
    2 x 400-g/14-oz. cans
    of cannellini beans
    in water, drained
    and rinsed
2 sage leaves (if using
    dried beans)
2 anchovy fillets
1 garlic clove, chopped
12 g/2 sprigs fresh
    parsley
6 tablespoons olive oil,
    plus extra for serving
1 teaspoon Dijon
    mustard
juice and grated zest
    of 1 lemon
150 g/5 oz. white/
    cup mushrooms,
    thinly sliced
150 g/5 oz. canned
    tuna in olive oil,
    drained
1 tablespoon finely
    chopped red onion
    or shallot
salt and freshly ground
    black pepper

SERVES 4

If using dried cannellini beans, soak them in cold water overnight or for 8 hours. Drain, then place in a large saucepan with the sage leaves. Cover with cold water and season with salt. Bring to the boil, skimming off any scum. Reduce the heat and simmer for 1 hour until the beans are tender; drain and set aside to cool.

Make a dressing by blitzing together the anchovy fillets, garlic, parsley (reserving a little for garnishing), olive oil, mustard and lemon juice in a food processor until smooth.

Toss the cooked cannellini beans with the dressing and place in a serving dish. Fold in two-thirds of the sliced mushrooms. Top with chunks of tuna and the remaining mushroom slices. Drizzle with a little olive oil, sprinkle with the reserved chopped parsley, red onion and lemon zest. Season with freshly ground black pepper and serve.

MUSHROOM, GOAT'S CHEESE AND LENTIL SALAD

When you don't want to spend too long in the kitchen, this is ideal. It draws on store-cupboard staples – lentils, olive oil, mustard and vinegar – to create a tasty meal. Adding raw mushrooms, soft, tangy goat's cheese, fresh herbs and lemon zest gives a lovely lift to the whole dish, making it perfect for warm-weather eating.

100 g/½ cup Puy/ French green lentils

3 tablespoons olive oil, plus extra for serving

1 tablespoon balsamic or red wine vinegar

1 teaspoon Dijon mustard

7 g/1–2 sprigs parsley, finely chopped

250 g/8 oz. white/cup mushrooms, sliced ½-cm/³⁄₁₆-inch thick

150 g/5 oz. soft goat's cheese, crumbled

2 tablespoons freshly chopped mint leaves

grated zest of 1 lemon

salt and freshly ground black pepper

SERVES 4

Rinse the lentils, then place in a saucepan and cover generously with cold water. Bring to the boil, then reduce the heat and simmer for 15 minutes until tender; drain.

While the lentils are cooking, mix together the olive oil, vinegar and mustard, seasoning with salt and freshly ground black pepper. Toss the warm lentils with the dressing, then set aside to cool.

Toss the lentils with the parsley and place in a salad serving bowl. Top with sliced mushrooms and goat's cheese. Sprinkle with mint and lemon zest. Dress with a little more olive oil and serve at once.

WILD MUSHROOM CARPACCIO

250 g/8 oz. assorted
  wild mushrooms
  or a mixture of these
  and cultivated
  mushrooms
1 garlic clove, finely
  chopped
4 tablespoons extra-
  virgin olive oil
3 tablespoons finely
  chopped fresh parsley
12 Parmesan shavings
salt and freshly ground
  black pepper

SERVES 4

This elegant dish is an easy way to showcase the flavour and texture of wild mushrooms when they are in season. Be sure to use the freshest mushrooms that you can find.

Trim and finely slice the wild mushrooms. Arrange them in overlapping slices on a serving platter. Season with salt and freshly ground black pepper.

Sprinkle with garlic and pour over the olive oil. Top with parsley and Parmesan shavings and serve at once.

FUNGI FOLKLORE

Mushrooms have always occupied a special place in our popular imagination, being thought of as otherworldly, or possessing uncanny powers. The way they spring up suddenly and mysteriously, has – no doubt – contributed to their mystique. The ancient Egyptians believed that wild mushrooms grew where lightning struck. In Europe, the sense that they come from another, supernatural world manifests itself in art, where paintings or drawings of fairies or gnomes often portray them sitting on or living in mushrooms.

Fairy rings or elf rings – the striking, naturally occurring circles or arcs of mushrooms, which are found growing in fields or forests – have long been thought of as magical places. They vary considerably in size, with some measuring hundreds of meters in diameter, and some are known to be centuries old. In England, it was thought that they were created by fairies dancing in a circle. In other European countries, there is similar folklore attached to them, as names such as the French *ronds de sorcières* (sorcerers' rings) or the German *hexenringe* (witches' rings) make clear. In many countries, it was thought dangerous to enter a fairy ring, particularly on a moonlit night, as the fairies, or other spirits, who use it might whisk you away. Or you might become trapped in the ring for having dared to enter. In Germany, where witches were thought to create the rings through dancing, they were regarded as particularly perilous on Walpurgisnacht, the night of April 30th, when witches were supposed to congregate. In Scotland, it was thought to be unlucky to till the land where a fairy ring was growing. In Wales, a mushroom ring signified the presence of a fairy community underground. Nowadays, we know fairy rings to be natural formations, created by the way in which mushrooms grow. Fairy rings in forests are known as 'tethered', because they

Mushrooms have long been attributed with mysterious, magical powers

Lingzhi mushrooms (*Ganoderma Lucidum*)

depend on a tree at their centre for their food. Mushroom circles without trees at their heart are known as 'free' circles. Around 60 species of mushrooms have the capacity to form fairy rings, the best-known being *Marasmius oreades*, popularly known as the 'fairy ring mushroom'.

The phrase 'magic mushrooms', of course, refers to the hallucinogenic properties of certain species. Over 180 different mushroom species contain psychedelic compounds psilocybin and psilocin. The eating of these fungi triggers experiences such as visions, feelings of euphoria and changes in perception. Archaeological evidence suggests that these psychedelic mushrooms were used thousands of years ago in ancient cultures in Mesoamerica during rituals. People's fascination with experimenting with ways of altering consciousness ensures a continued interest in psychedelic mushrooms.

Another reason for our fascination with mushrooms rests with the potential peril presented by wild mushrooms. Around 70–80 species are poisonous,

among then *Amanita Muscaria*, the classic white-spotted red toadstool portrayed in children's stories. Among the superstitions attached to wild mushrooms was the belief that picking them at the wrong time of the month, when the moon wasn't full, caused them to become poisonous.

In contrast, mushrooms have also been thought to have beneficial powers. In Ancient Egypt, it was believed that wild mushrooms conferred immortality, with the eating of them reserved as a privilege for the Pharaoh. For thousands of years, mushrooms have been used in traditional Chinese medicine. In both China and Japan, the eating of certain mushroom varieties is thought to maintain good health and promote longevity. The reishi mushroom (*Ganoderma lucidum*), known as Lingzhi, has long been particularly valued for its healthy qualities, traditionally prepared in a tea. Recent years have seen scientific research carried out on reishi, investigating areas such as its ability to renew the liver, its anti-carcinogenic properties and lifespan-extending polysaccharides.

MUSHROOM AND SEAWEED NOODLE SALAD

180 g/6 oz. egg
    noodles or soba
    noodles
200 g/6½ oz. assorted
    exotic mushrooms
    (shiitake, eryngi,
    oyster, shiro shimeji)
10 g/⅓ oz. dried
    wakame, soaked
    in warm water for
    5 minutes
75 g/⅔ cup frozen
    edamame/soya
    beans, cooked
    and drained
a thumb-sized piece of
    root ginger, shredded
1 spring onion/scallion,
    finely chopped, white
    and green separated
1 tablespoon sesame
    seeds, plus extra
    for serving

DRESSING
100 ml/6 tablespoons
    dashi stock
2 tablespoons mirin
3 tablespoons light
    soy sauce
1 tablespoon sesame
    seed oil

SERVES 4

With its Japanese-inspired combination of subtle flavours and textures, this makes a stylish noodle dish, served at room temperature and ideal for either lunch or dinner. For maximum visual impact, use as varied a mixture of fresh exotic mushrooms as you can find.

Cook the noodles following the instructions on the packet until al dente; drain and then plunge into cold water. Drain once more.

Trim the assorted mushrooms, slicing any larger ones.

Mix together all of the dressing ingredients in a small bowl. Toss together the cooked noodles, wakame, edamame, root ginger, whites of the spring onion/scallion and dressing. Toss with the sesame seeds. Toss two-thirds of the mushrooms through the noodles. Top with the remaining mushrooms, sprinkle with the green spring onion/scallion and serve at once.

PUY LENTILS WITH
MUSHROOMS AND SQUASH

An earthy combination of flavours and textures makes this a satisfying vegetarian dish. Serve with quinoa, sweet potato mash or roasted root vegetables for a hearty meal.

15 g/½ oz. assorted dried mushrooms (morels, porcini, girolles)
200 ml/¾ cup hot water
120 g/⅔ cup Puy/ French green lentils
1 tablespoon olive oil
1 red onion, sliced
1 garlic clove, chopped
1 celery stalk, finely chopped
1 rosemary sprig, leaves only
1 x 400-g/14-oz. can of chopped tomatoes
a pinch of sugar
400 g/14 oz. (1 small) butternut squash, peeled and cubed
200 g/6½ oz. chestnut/cremini mushrooms, halved
salt and freshly ground black pepper
chopped parsley, to garnish

SERVES 4

Soak the dried mushrooms in the hot water for 20 minutes. Strain, reserving the mushrooms and 100 ml/scant ½ cup of the soaking water.

Place the lentils in a pan and cover with cold water. Bring to the boil, then reduce the heat and simmer for 20–25 minutes until the lentils have softened, but retain some texture; drain and set aside until needed.

Heat the olive oil in a casserole dish or Dutch oven over a medium heat. Fry the onion, garlic, celery and rosemary for 2–3 minutes until softened and fragrant. Add the chopped tomatoes. Season with salt, pepper and sugar. Bring to the boil. Add the butternut squash and the reserved soaking water from the dried mushrooms. Cover and cook over a medium heat for 10 minutes, until the squash is tender.

Mix in the soaked dry mushrooms, chestnut/cremini mushrooms and cooked lentils. Cover and cook for 5 minutes. Check the seasoning. Garnish with parsley and serve at once.

MUSHROOM AND AVOCADO WRAPS

With their fresh, clean flavours, these tasty vegetarian wraps are great for a light meal.

25 g/1 small bunch fresh coriander/cilantro
3 tablespoons extra-virgin olive oil
freshly squeezed juice of ½ lemon
300 g/10 oz. white/cup mushrooms, thinly sliced
2 ripe avocados
4 large tortilla wraps/flour tortillas
4 tablespoons sour cream
salt and freshly ground black pepper

SERVES 4

Blitz together the coriander/cilantro, olive oil and lemon juice (reserving 1 teaspoon of lemon juice for the avocados) into a paste. Season with salt and freshly ground black pepper.

Toss the mushroom slices with the coriander/cilantro paste. Peel and slice the avocados, tossing the slices with the reserved lemon juice to prevent them discolouring.

Spread each tortilla wrap with about 1 tablespoon each of sour cream. Top with the mushroom and avocado slices and roll the wraps up over the filling. Serve at once.

MUSHROOM BURGERS

Creamy Camembert cheese pairs well with mushrooms in this flavourful, vegetarian take on a classic hamburger.

2 tablespoons olive oil
1 large red onion, halved and thinly sliced
2 fresh thyme sprigs
¼ teaspoon white sugar
1 teaspoon balsamic vinegar
2 teaspoons butter
2 large, flat mushrooms, stalks removed
salt and freshly ground black pepper

TO SERVE (OPTIONAL)
burger buns, halved
mayonnaise
iceberg lettuce
thin slices of Camembert

SERVES 2

Heat 1 tablespoon of the olive oil in a large, heavy frying pan/skillet. Add the red onion and thyme and fry gently over a low heat for 8 minutes, stirring now and then, until softened. Add the sugar and vinegar and fry for 2 minutes more until caramelized. Set aside.

Wipe the frying pan/skillet clean. Heat the remaining 1 tablespoon olive oil and butter over a medium heat. Add the mushrooms and fry for 5 minutes, turning often, until browned on both sides. Season with salt and freshly ground black pepper.

Briefly grill/broil the burger buns, cut-side up, until just golden. Spread the bottom half with mayonnaise. Layer lettuce, a mushroom, Camembert cheese and half the caramelized onions in each bun. Serve at once.

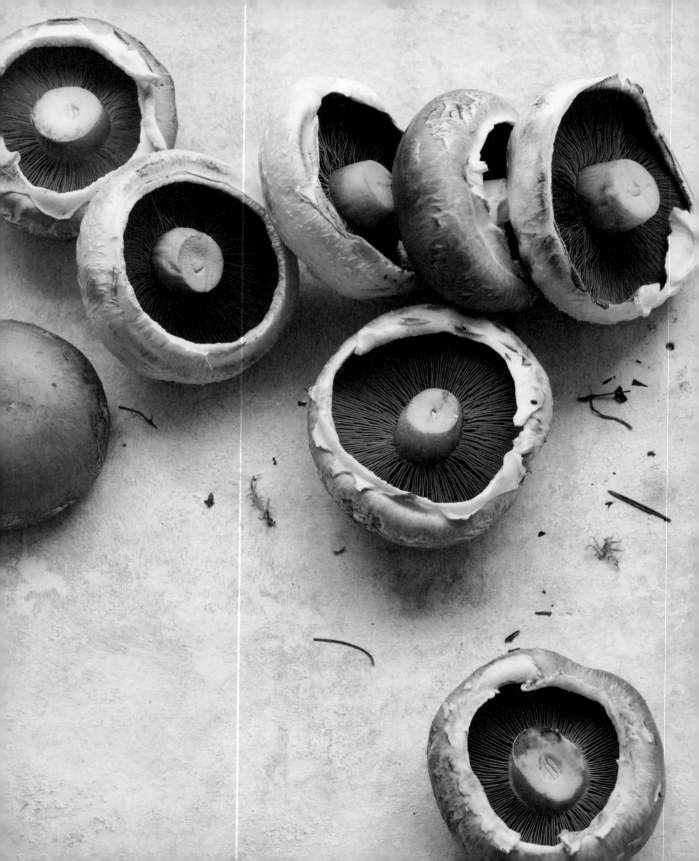

MUSHROOM-STUFFED RED PEPPERS

Halved red (bell) peppers make colourful, natural cases for a tasty mushroom filling. Serve as an appetizer for a dinner party. Alternatively, for a vegetarian main course for two, allow two stuffed pepper halves per serving, accompanying them with saffron rice and plain yogurt

1 tablespoon olive oil
1 shallot, finely chopped
½ celery stalk,
   finely chopped
200 g/6 oz. white/
   cup mushrooms,
   finely chopped
2 fresh sage leaves,
   shredded
1 teaspoon tomato
   paste
a handful of finely
   chopped parsley
grated zest of ½ lemon
1 tablespoon pine nuts
2 tablespoons fresh
   breadcrumbs
25 g/⅓ cup Cheddar
   cheese, grated
2 large red (bell)
   peppers, deseeded
   and halved
salt and freshly ground
   black pepper

SERVES 4
AS AN APPETIZER

Preheat the oven to 200°C (400°F) Gas 6.

Prepare the filling. Heat the olive oil in a frying pan/skillet over a low–medium heat. Add the shallot and celery and fry gently, until softened. Add the mushrooms and sage and fry, stirring often, until the mushrooms have softened. Mix in the tomato paste, chopped parsley and lemon zest and season with salt and pepper.

Remove from the heat and mix in the pine nuts, breadcrumbs and Cheddar cheese.

Place the four red (bell) pepper halves on a baking sheet. Divide the mushroom stuffing among the pepper halves.

Bake in the preheated oven for 30 minutes. Serve at once.

SAUTÉED POTATOES
WITH CHANTERELLES

Wild mushrooms are one of the year's seasonal pleasures. To enjoy
them at their best, you often only need to cook them simply and briefly.
This recipe transforms classic sautéed potatoes into a luxurious treat.

**100 g/3½ oz.
chanterelles**
2 tablespoons olive oil
**600 g/1¼ lb. waxy
potatoes, boiled,
peeled, sliced 1-cm/
³⁄₈-inch thick**
1 shallot, finely chopped
**salt and freshly ground
black pepper**
**freshly chopped parsley,
to garnish**

SERVES 4

Carefully trim the chanterelles
and cut any large ones in half.
Set aside.

Heat 1 tablespoon of the olive oil
in a large, heavy-based frying
pan/skillet. Add the potato slices
in a single layer and fry over a
medium heat, until golden-brown
underneath, turn, and fry for
5 minutes more.

Add the remaining 1 tablespoon
of olive oil to the pan, heat
through and add the shallot.
Fry until softened. Add the
chanterelles and fry, stirring, for
2–3 minutes until just softened.
Season with salt and freshly
ground black pepper. Serve
at once, garnished with the
chopped parsley.

MUSHROOM PARMIGIANA

This version of a classic, much-loved Italian aubergine/eggplant dish is given extra savoury richness by the addition of a generous amount of mushrooms. Usefully, it can be made ahead, then baked as needed. Serve it simply with a crisp-textured green salad – which contrasts well – and steamed rice, to soak up the juices.

4–6 tablespoons olive oil

1 onion, peeled and finely chopped

1 garlic clove, peeled and finely chopped

1 anchovy fillet, chopped

1 x 400-g/14-oz. can of chopped tomatoes

2 pinches of chilli flakes/hot red pepper flakes

a generous pinch of dried oregano

2 aubergines/ eggplants, thinly sliced lengthways

600 g/20 oz. large white/cup mushrooms, sliced 1-cm/⅜-inch thick

2 balls of mozzarella cheese, drained and cut into chunks

2–3 tablespoons fresh breadcrumbs

2 tablespoons finely grated Parmesan

salt and freshly ground black pepper

SERVES 4–6

First, make the tomato sauce. Heat a tablespoon of the oil in a saucepan. Add the onion and garlic and fry for 2–3 minutes over a medium heat, until softened and fragrant. Add the anchovy fillet and fry until it has melted in. Add the chopped tomatoes, chilli flakes/ hot red pepper flakes and oregano. Season with salt and freshly ground black pepper. Bring to the boil, then reduce the heat and simmer for 10 minutes, stirring now and then. Blend the tomato sauce using a stick blender or food processor.

Preheat the oven to 200°C (400°F) Gas 6.

Heat 2 tablespoons of the olive oil in a large, non-stick frying pan/skillet. Fry the aubergine/ eggplant slices in batches, over a medium heat, until softened and browned on both sides, adding in more oil if needed. Remove from the pan and set aside.

Heat 1 tablespoon of the olive oil in the same frying pan/skillet. Add the mushrooms and fry over a medium heat for 2 minutes on each side, until lightly browned.

Spread a spoonful of the tomato sauce over the base of a shallow oven-proof dish. Top with a layer of fried aubergine/eggplant. Spread 1–2 tablespoons tomato sauce evenly over the aubergine/ eggplant, then add a layer of fried mushrooms, then sprinkle a few mozzarella chunks. Repeat the layering process, finishing with a generous layer of sauce and, finally, a topping of breadcrumbs and Parmesan.

Bake in the preheated oven for 40 minutes, until the breadcrumbs and Parmesan are golden brown. Serve hot from the oven, warm or at room temperature; it tastes good at any of these temperatures!

EGGS AND CHEESE

BAKED MUSHROOM AND EGG RAMEKINS

Mushrooms and eggs have a delicious affinity – their delicate flavours complementing each other, rather than overpowering. This traditional egg dish is given a luxurious touch by adding a layer of fried mushrooms. A hint of tarragon adds a pleasing aniseed note. Serve with toast fingers for brunch, or with bread rolls as an appetizer.

1 tablespoon olive oil
½ onion, finely chopped
400 g/14 oz. white/
  cup mushrooms,
  thinly sliced
2 tablespoons freshly
  chopped tarragon
  leaves, plus extra
  to garnish
4 eggs
4 tablespoons double/
  heavy cream
4 tablespoons grated
  Parmesan cheese
salt and freshly ground
  black pepper
4 ramekins

SERVES 4

Preheat oven to 180°C (350°F) Gas 4.

Heat the olive oil in a frying pan/skillet. Fry the onion over a low heat, until softened. Add the mushrooms, increase the heat, and fry briefly until the mushrooms are softened. Mix in the tarragon, season with salt and freshly ground black pepper, and cook for a further 2 minutes.

Divide the mushroom mixture between the 4 ramekin dishes.

Break an egg into the centre of each ramekin. Season the eggs with salt and freshly ground black pepper. Pour a tablespoon of double/heavy cream over each egg, then sprinkle each with Parmesan cheese.

Bake in the preheated oven for 8–10 minutes for runny yolks, or 15–20 minutes for set yolks. Garnish with tarragon and serve warm from the oven.

MUSHROOM AND HALLOUMI KEBABS

With their natural bouncy texture, mushrooms lend themselves to being grilled/broiled or barbecued. Pleasingly plump button mushrooms, salty halloumi cheese and juicy cherry tomatoes combine well, offering a taste of the Mediterranean. Cook over a barbecue for extra flavour. Serve with a rocket/arugula, cucumber and tomato salad.

250 g/8 oz. halloumi
cheese, cut into
16 even-sized pieces
16 even-sized button
mushrooms, stalks
trimmed off
12 cherry tomatoes
2 tablespoons olive oil
1 tablespoon freshly
chopped parsley
leaves
8 fresh bay leaves,
stalks trimmed,
halved
8 thin lemon slices
salt and freshly ground
black pepper
8 metal cooking
skewers

SERVES 4

Preheat the grill/broiler.

In a large bowl, toss together the halloumi cheese, button mushrooms, cherry tomatoes, olive oil and parsley. Season with salt and freshly ground black pepper, bearing in mind the natural saltiness of the halloumi.

Thread the cheese, mushrooms, cherry tomatoes, bay leaves and lemon slices onto the 8 skewers.

Grill/broil the halloumi skewers for 5 minutes, turning over halfway through, until the halloumi is golden-brown. Serve at once.

SCRAMBLED EGGS WITH CHANTERELLES

This simple but luxurious combination makes a wonderful breakfast or brunch dish.

100 g/3½ oz. fresh chanterelle mushrooms
4 eggs
1 tablespoon butter, plus extra for the toast
1 tablespoon olive oil
2 slices of freshly made toast
salt and freshly ground black pepper
freshly chopped parsley, to garnish (optional)

SERVES 2

Trim down the stalks of the chanterelle mushrooms and halve any large ones.

Beat the eggs together in a bowl and season with salt and freshly ground black pepper.

Heat the butter in small, heavy saucepan. Add the beaten egg and cook over a low heat, stirring often, until scrambled.

Meanwhile, heat the olive oil in a frying pan/skillet. Add the chanterelles and fry over a high heat for 2–3 minutes, until lightly browned and softened. Season with salt and freshly ground black pepper.

Spread the toast with butter, top with the scrambled eggs and then the fried chanterelles. Serve at once, garnished with freshly chopped parsley.

TRICOLORE MUSHROOM FRITTATA

A frittata – the Italian version of an omelette – offers an excellent though simple meal. Flexibly, it can be served either freshly made or at room temperature. A mixture of mushrooms, onions, sun-dried tomatoes and artichokes gives body and flavour to this savoury egg dish. Serve it with a fresh salad on the side for a light lunch or supper.

2 tablespoons olive oil
½ red onion, chopped
½ red (bell) pepper, cut into short 1-cm/ ³⁄₈-inch-thick strips
150 g/5 oz. white/cup mushrooms, halved
50 g/3 artichokes in oil, well-drained and chopped
4 sun-dried tomatoes in oil, chopped
6 eggs
2 tablespoons grated Parmesan cheese
a handful of fresh basil leaves, roughly torn
2 tablespoons butter
salt and freshly ground black pepper
a 25-cm/10-inch heavy-based frying pan/skillet

SERVES 4

Heat the olive oil over a medium heat in a frying pan/skillet. Fry the onion and red (bell) pepper for 3 minutes, until softened. Add the mushrooms and fry for 3 minutes. Remove from the pan; set aside to cool. When cool, mix together with the artichokes and sun-dried tomatoes. Wipe the pan clean.

Thoroughly whisk the eggs together in a mixing bowl. Season with salt and freshly ground black pepper. Mix in the Parmesan, the cooled vegetable mixture and the basil leaves.

Heat the butter in the frying pan/skillet over a medium heat, until frothing. Add the egg mixture, spreading it to form an even layer. Reduce the heat to low and cook for 15–20 minutes, until the base of the frittata has set, but the surface is still liquid.

Preheat the grill/broiler. Place the frittata under the grill/broiler for 1–2 minutes until the surface has set. Serve warm or at room temperature, in slices.

MUSHROOM AND POTATO GRATIN WITH GRUYÈRE

A luxurious take on a classic potato gratin, given an umami richness by the addition of mushrooms and Gruyère cheese. A great dinner party dish, this is an excellent accompaniment for a rich beef stew.

25 g/1 oz. dried
  mushrooms (a
  mixture of morels,
  trompette, girolle
  and porcini)
900 g/2 lbs. waxy
  potatoes, peeled
300 ml/1¼ cups full
  fat/whole milk
300 ml/1¼ cups
  double/heavy cream
a sprig of thyme
1 garlic clove, chopped
freshly grated nutmeg
1 tablespoon olive oil
1 shallot, finely chopped
250 g/8 oz. fresh white/
  cup mushrooms,
  thinly sliced
1 tablespoon butter
150 g/5 oz. Gruyère
  cheese, thinly sliced
salt and freshly ground
  black pepper

SERVES 6

Soak the dried mushrooms in hot water for 20 minutes; drain and discard the liquid.

Finely slice the potatoes. Bring the milk, double/heavy cream, thyme and garlic to the boil in a saucepan. Season with salt and freshly ground black pepper and nutmeg. Add the potato slices and simmer for 10 minutes.

Preheat the oven to 180°C (350°F) Gas 4.

Meanwhile, heat the olive oil in a frying pan/skillet. Add the shallot and fry over a low heat, stirring, for 2 minutes. Add the sliced mushrooms. Increase the heat to high and fry for 3 minutes, stirring, until the mushrooms are lightly browned. Add the soaked dried mushrooms. Season with salt and freshly ground black pepper.

In a shallow, ovenproof dish, arrange a third of the creamy potato mixture in a layer at the bottom of the dish. Top with half of the Gruyère slices and then a layer of the mushroom mixture. Repeat the layers, then finish with the last of the potato mixture. Dot the surface with butter. Bake in the preheated oven for 50–60 minutes, until golden-brown. Serve hot from the oven.

GLORIOUS TRUFFLES

Despite their unassuming appearance, truffles – the fruiting bodies of an underground fungus – have long been prized as an intriguing, rare luxury. The ancient Greeks attributed aphrodisiac powers to them. Their origins were considered mysterious – the Greek essayist Plutarch (46–120 AD) thought that lightning strikes gave rise to them. The Romans enjoyed a particular desert truffle, Terfezia, which they imported from Arab lands. Of the 70 truffle varieties, just two are particularly highly prized: *Tuber melanosporum*, the black truffle of Périgord, France, and *Tuber magnatum*, the white truffle of Alba, Italy. It is in these two countries that truffles

are particularly revered. The French gastronome Brillat-Savarin declared the truffle to be the 'diamond of cookery', while the French novelist Alexandre Dumas wrote: 'When I eat truffles, I become livelier, happier.' These two esteemed truffles are harvested in the late autumn/fall through to winter and are noted for their distinctive, powerful aromas. Because of this, dishes using them are often simple, designed to showcase this seasonal treat. In Italy, for example, one might be served a dish of fresh tagliatelle, tossed with butter and Parmesan, topped with fresh truffle shavings, often shaved at the table in front of the diner. In France, truffles are used both raw and

Daniel Chaume and his truffle-hunting pig, Ninnie, Perigord, France

cooked, in an array of quintessential recipes, from sauces to meat dishes. Pieces of truffle are used to stud pâtés, terrines and foie gras, imparting their flavour to these charcuterie classics. One renowned, classic French recipe for truffles is the great chef Escoffier's recipe for *Truffes sous la cendre* sees whole truffles wrapped in pork fat and waxed paper and baked in ashes.

The best fresh truffles command famously high prices. As one might expect, there have long been attempts to cultivate truffles, in order to take advantage of what would be a lucrative crop. The way in which truffles grow, however, proves a barrier to commercially viable cultivation. It takes 7–10 years before truffles bear their fruiting bodies and the investment required in order to control and maintain a 'truffle plantation' are high. Adding to the mystique of truffles, therefore, is the fact that they are largely foraged. As they grow underground, keen-scented dogs, known as truffle hounds, and also pigs, which have a great sense of smell, are used to sniff them out. These animals are carefully trained and highly prized by their owners. The thrills of truffle hunting in the wild are considerable; a large truffle can be worth a small fortune to its owner.

For a memorable, truffle-infused experience, head to the Fiera del Tartufo (Truffle Fair) held annually during October and November in Alba, Piedmont, Italy. The countryside around Alba is famed for its white truffles, so is an apt location for this event. Over the decades, famous visitors to the region have been presented with white truffles. In 1951, a truly splendid truffle, weighing a magnificent 2.52 kg/5½ lbs., was presented to US President Truman. The fair offers visitors a chance to sample truffles in numerous forms, to buy directly from truffle hunters and enjoy some fine local wine.

If you do buy a fresh truffle, then be sure to look after it properly. It should be brushed clean, dried thoroughly and stored in an airtight container in the fridge. One traditional way of making the most of a fresh truffle is to store it with eggs for 2–3 days, again in an airtight container in the fridge, so that the scent permeates the eggs, which can then be used to make extremely indulgent scrambled eggs! Alternatively, surround the truffle with risotto rice, store in the fridge, and then use that rice to make a superb risotto. While fresh truffles are rare and very expensive, a good quality truffle oil is an affordable and handy option. I've used it to add that touch of truffle flavour in recipes such as my dangerously addictive Truffled Fries (page 84), Truffled Roast Chicken (page 88) and Truffled Mushroom Lasagne (page 79). Only a little is needed – it goes a long way!

MUSHROOM FILO PIE

One of the charms of mushrooms is their versatility as an ingredient. Here, they are used to create a fungi-based version of a classic Greek spinach pie. Crisp, buttery layers of filo/phyllo pastry contrast nicely with a soft, savoury mushroom and feta cheese filling. Serve warm from the oven or at room temperature, accompanied by a green salad.

1 tablespoon olive oil
4 spring onions/
    scallions, finely
    chopped
700 g/1¾ lb. white/
    cup mushrooms,
    thinly sliced
3 eggs, beaten
200 g/6½ oz. feta
    cheese
25 g/3–4 sprigs fresh
    dill, finely chopped
2 tablespoons pine nuts
    (optional)
300 g/10 oz. filo/phyllo
    pastry
75 g/5 tablespoons
    butter, melted
salt and freshly ground
    black pepper
*a greased 23-cm/9-inch
    square baking pan*

SERVES 4–6

Heat the olive oil in large frying pan/skillet. Add the spring onions/scallions and fry over a low heat for 1 minute, until softened. Add the mushrooms and season with salt and pepper. Fry over a high heat for 15–20 minutes, stirring often, until the mushrooms are browned and the excess moisture has been cooked off. Set aside to cool.

Preheat the oven to 200°C (400°F) Gas 6.

Beat the eggs in a mixing bowl. Crumble in the feta cheese. Season with salt and pepper, bearing in mind the saltiness of the feta. Mix in the cooled mushrooms, dill and pine nuts.

Brush a pastry sheet generously with melted butter (keeping the remaining filo/phyllo sheets covered with cling film/plastic wrap or a clean kitchen cloth so they don't dry out). Press the buttered filo sheet into the greased baking pan, tucking the edges in around the sides. Repeat the buttering pastry process, adding layers until half of the pastry has been used, forming a pastry case.

Spread the mushroom mixture evenly in the middle of the case. Top the mushroom mixture with more layers of buttered filo/phyllo pastry, tucking the edges in to form a covered pie. Brush the top pastry layer generously with melted butter.

Bake in the preheated oven for 40–45 minutes until golden-brown. Cut into wedges to serve.

MUSHROOM AND PARMA HAM PIZZA

Making home-made pizza from scratch is great fun and very satisfying. It also means that you can be creative with the toppings! The additions of Parma ham/prosciutto and a touch of truffle oil make for a stylish take on a mushroom pizza. Serve the pizzas warm, with a spinach and tomato salad on the side, for a great savoury meal.

500 g/4 cups strong white/bread flour
1 teaspoon quick dried/rapid-rise yeast
1 teaspoon salt
½ teaspoon sugar
250–275 ml/1–1¼ cups warm water
3½ tablespoons olive oil
500 g/2 lbs. white/cup mushrooms, sliced ½-cm/³⁄₁₆-inch thick
1 garlic clove, chopped
2 balls of mozzarella cheese, torn into pieces
4 slices of Parma ham/prosciutto, roughly torn
freshly chopped parsley, to garnish
1 teaspoon truffle oil (optional)
salt and freshly ground black pepper
pizza stones (optional)

MAKES 4

First, make the pizza dough. Place the flour, yeast, salt and sugar in a large bowl and mix together. Gradually mix in the warm water to form a soft, sticky dough. Knead the dough on a floured surface for 10 minutes, until smooth and supple.

Place the dough in a floured bowl, cover with a clean kitchen cloth or cling film/plastic wrap. Set aside in a warm place for 1 hour to rise, until the dough has doubled in size.

Preheat the oven to 250°C (475°F) Gas 9. Place the pizza stones, if using, or baking sheets in the oven to preheat.

Heat a large, heavy frying pan/skillet. Add 1 tablespoon of the olive oil, heat through, then add the mushrooms. Fry over a high heat for 8 minutes, stirring now and then, until any liquid from the mushrooms has evaporated and they are lightly browned. Add a further ½ tablespoon olive oil and heat through. Add the garlic to the oil and fry, stirring, for 1 minute. Season with salt and pepper. Set aside.

Divide the risen dough into 4 equal-sized portions. Roll out each portion on a lightly floured, clean work surface, to form a circular pizza base. Brush each pizza base evenly with ½ tablespoon of the olive oil. Sprinkle each with the fried mushrooms, dividing them evenly among the 4 bases. Dot with mozzarella pieces.

Transfer to the hot pizza stones, if using, or hot baking sheets, then bake the pizzas, in batches if necessary, in the preheated oven for 10 minutes until the dough is golden-brown.

Top the pizzas with Parma ham/prosciutto and sprinkle with parsley. Drizzle ¼ tablespoon truffle oil over each pizza, if using. Serve at once.

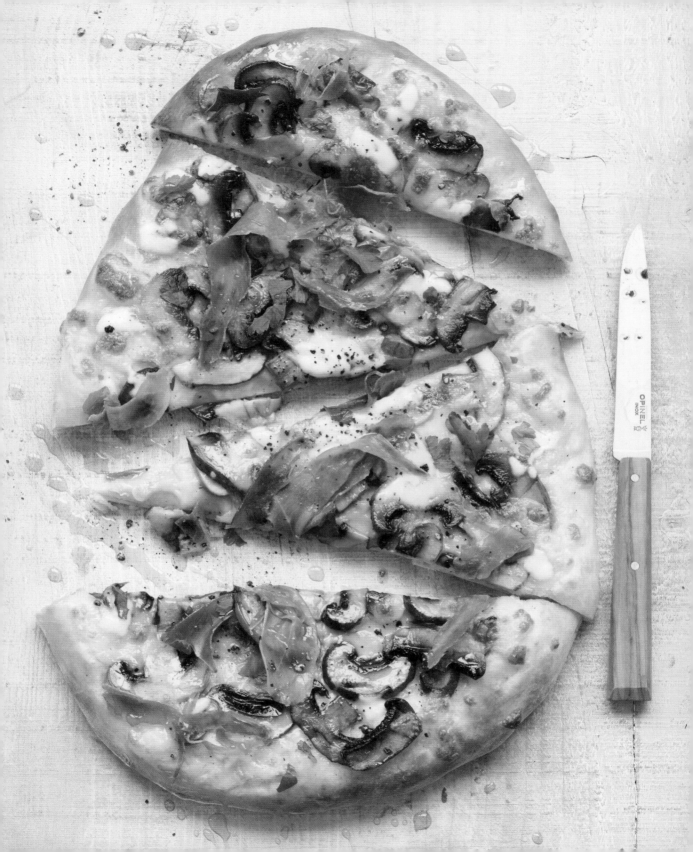

MUSHROOM, BLUE CHEESE AND WALNUT QUICHE

Mushroom quiche is a much-loved classic. In this version, a nutty-tasting spelt flour crust encases a rich filling made from fried mushrooms and shallots, combined with savoury blue cheese. Stylish enough for entertaining, this can be baked in advance and served at room temperature. Serve with a refreshing watercress or radicchio salad for contrast.

150 g/1 cup plus 3 tablespoons spelt flour
75 g/5 tablespoons butter
1 tablespoon olive oil
1 shallot, chopped
300 g/10 oz. white/cup mushrooms, sliced 1-cm/⅜-inch thick
300 g/1¼ cups double/heavy cream
2 whole eggs
1 egg yolk
freshly grated nutmeg
100 g/3½ oz. blue cheese, crumbled into small chunks
50 g/⅓ cup walnut pieces
salt and freshly ground black pepper
24-cm/9½-inch loose-based quiche/flan pan, lightly greased
baking beans

MAKES 1 QUICHE

Place the flour, a pinch of salt and the butter in a food processor. Pulse until the butter has been absorbed by the flour. Add 2 tablespoons cold water and blend until the mixture comes together to form a pastry. Cover with cling film/plastic wrap and chill for 30 minutes.

Heat the olive oil in a frying pan/skillet. Fry the shallot over a medium heat for 2 minutes, until softened. Add the mushrooms and fry over a high heat, until lightly browned. Drain in a colander and allow to cool.

Preheat the oven to 200°C (400°F) Gas 6.

Make the pastry case. Roll out the pastry thinly on a lightly floured work surface. Line the greased pan with the pastry, pressing it in firmly. Prick the base several times with a fork, to stop the pastry bubbling up. Line the case with baking parchment and fill with baking beans. Blind bake the pastry case in the preheated oven for 15 minutes. Carefully remove the baking parchment and beans and bake for a further 5 minutes, then remove from the oven. Leave the oven on.

Meanwhile, whisk together the double/heavy cream, whole eggs and egg yolk. Season with salt, freshly ground black pepper and grated nutmeg.

Sprinkle the blue cheese and walnuts in an even layer inside the pastry case. Top with the fried mushrooms and pour over the cream mixture. Bake for 40 minutes. Remove, allow to cool slightly, and serve warm or at room temperature.

INDEX

PICTURE CREDITS

All photography by Clare Winfield apart from pages:
26l Fotografia Basica/Getty Images
26c Dorling Kindersley/Getty Images
26r Mike Berceanu/Getty Images
27 gutaper/Getty Images
48l Fred Bruemmer/Getty Images
48r Andia/UIG via Getty Images
49l Matt Meadows/Getty Images
49c Wilfried Martin/Getty Images
49r Alan Tunnicliffe Photography/Getty Images
72l Jason Ingrams/National Trust
72r Paul Pellegrino/iStock /Getty Images
73 Kate Whitaker

96l Gary Smith/Getty Images
96r Seth Joel/Getty Images
97l Aleksandar Milutinovic/Getty Images
97c Karnauhov/Getty Images
97r BruceBlock/Getty Images
122l dabjola/Getty Images
122r Tony Wharton/Getty Images
123l ukjent/Getty Images
123r tinglee1631/Getty Images
150 Caroline Blumberg/Bloomberg via Getty
Images
151 Renault Philippe/Getty Images

ACKNOWLEDGEMENTS

My thanks go to my family and friends, who gave me feedback and support as I tested the mushroom recipes for the book.

Many thanks also to the brilliant Sous Chef (www.souschef.co.uk) for their generous support sourcing and sampling interesting dried mushrooms. Thanks, too, to the always helpful John and Elena at Puntarelle & Co and Parkway Greens. My thanks to expert mushroom farmers Cynan Jones of The Mushroom Garden, Jim Angelucci of Phillips Mushroom Farms and Noel Arnold of Li-Sun Exotic Mushrooms for letting me interview them for the book.

Creating a book is truly a team effort and working with RPS is always a pleasure. Thank you to Julia Charles and Cindy Richards for commissioning the idea and to Alice Sambrook for editing. I have really enjoyed exploring mushrooms for it! It's a lovely-looking book so thank you to Leslie Harrington and the team: Clare Winfield for her elegant photography, Matthew Ford for the food styling, Jennifer Kay for the props and Sonya Nathoo for art direction and design.

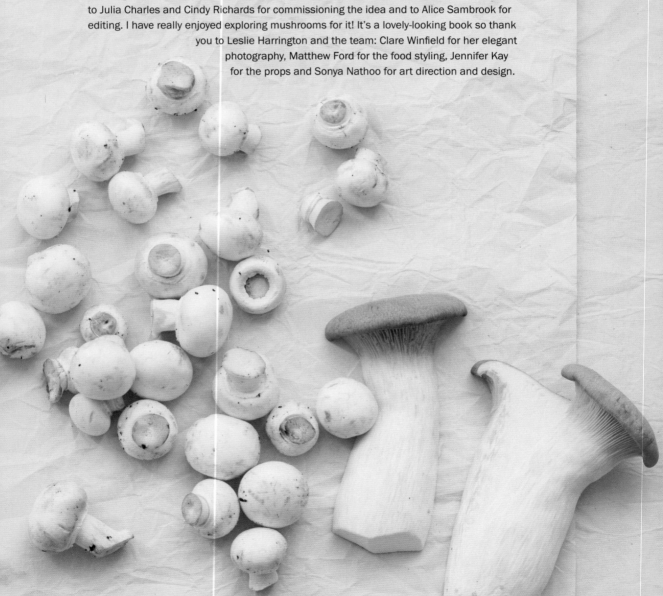